operating
on faith

Also by Matt Weber

Fearing the Stigmata

operating
on faith

A PAINFULLY TRUE LOVE STORY

MATT WEBER

LOYOLA PRESS.
A JESUIT MINISTRY
Chicago

LOYOLA PRESS.
A JESUIT MINISTRY

3441 N. Ashland Avenue
Chicago, Illinois 60657
(800) 621-1008
www.loyolapress.com

Cover art credit: Fancy Photography/Veer, Thinkstock/Photodisc/Ryan McVay, Thinkstock/
Stockbyte/George Doyle & Ciaran Griffin, Kite-Kit/Sutterstock

Back cover author photo, Jill Anderson.

ISBN-13: 978-0-8294-4409-4
ISBN-10: 0-8294-4409-2
Library of Congress Control Number: 2015955685

Printed in the United States of America.

16 17 18 19 20 21 22 Bang 10 9 8 7 6 5 4 3 2 1

For my darling Nell

"What matters in life is not what happens to you but what you remember and how you remember it."
—Gabriel García Márquez

Contents

Introduction

A quick warning before you proceed with reading—I do this out of respect for my very proper and dignified mother-in-law—there is a chapter in this book about the redemptive nature of flatulence. I promise you it is totally in context, canonically respectful, and imperative to the narrative of this story. If you are a fifteen-year-old boy, perhaps you wish to flip directly to this chapter (it's chapter 9). If you didn't just set this book down in polite objection, I thank you for your early commitment, and I promise to do my very best to make these words, well, not stink.

As you might have gathered, this is no ordinary introduction for a book sitting in the Christian or inspirational section of the bookstore. What you are about to read is neither extraordinary nor special, but simply a peculiar story about an individual whose first twenty-nine years of life were charmed, idyllic, halcyon—the sentimental stuff of *Leave It to Beaver* and *The Andy Griffith Show*—until they were abruptly preempted by a surprise mash-up of *ER*, *Jackass*, and *Desperate Housewives*.

This is the true story of me, Matt Weber, your typical, overeducated, flannel-wearing child of the nineties who once considered a slight alteration in the recipe for garlic knots at a restaurant near his house to be a terrible, horrible, no-good moment in his otherwise contented life. You are about to meet me in the first chapter of this book at my twenty-ninth birthday party, singing along with a pool-cleaning, middle-aged, Christian Elvis impersonator and feeling on top of the world. I then get married, buy a house, get a new job, adopt a rat-sized dog, start a national speaking tour, and gain twenty pounds from consuming an inordinate amount of mushroom pizza and Goldfish crackers.

And then, like any good reality TV show, it all comes crashing down. I burst at the seams—literally, like, burst open so that I require a five-hour emergency surgery, have 30 percent of my stomach removed, and need dozens of stitches and staples down my belly just to hold me together. Holding me together emotionally is my intrepid wife, Nell, fresh off taking a vow of "in sickness and in health" and showing me a depth and quality of love I never knew possible.

Spoiler alert: I survive the surgery, but my relationship with my body, my God, my wife, and the world becomes profoundly different. And I guess I'm now the type of person who isn't so stressed about beginning his later-than-usual Catholic coming-of-age book with fore-warnings about farts.

1

Twenty-nine Is the New Twenty-nine

I was pretty sure she was flirting with me from across the room. She was tallish but not tall, had sandy blonde hair, subtle blue eyes, and the perfect number of freckles on her face. I noticed the flicker of a diamond ring on her left hand as I smiled back at her. In situations like these, I stick with a closed-mouth smile to hedge against the possibility of exposing a tiny foreign object protruding from my 85 percent straight, 80 percent white teeth. She began to stride—nay, glide—toward me and my heart beat a little faster. As she approached, I couldn't help but notice my mother talking to Elvis and my father examining sheet music with pregnant twins in Renaissance garb.

The aroma of pizza was wafting into the family room, merging with the distinctive nasal flavors of cooling cheesy garlic bread. I'm usually easily distracted by the smells of Italian food, followed by a need to taste those aroma emanators, but in this particular instance, all of my energy was focused on my sense of sight—the sight of this beautiful woman just nearing my chair.

"Happy Birthday, Matty," she said with a tinge of the Texan drawl she denies having. "Are you enjoying your party?" Uncontrollably flashing some teeth in a big grin, I looked up at her and was compelled to answer with a kiss. I didn't care if Elvis or my parents saw—they would be observing a similar kiss in just a few months when I returned to Holy Rosary Parish in Houston, Texas, to marry this girl.

"I'm glad," said Eleanor Barron O'Donnell, my fiancée of almost five months. "My mother was really excited when she found out her pool guy was also an Elvis impersonator."

It was October 4, 2012, my 29th birthday, and I was glad my parents took two very inconvenient, early morning connections from Massachusetts to get to this party. I rarely have the chance to see them on my actual birthday, and I was excited (albeit nervous) for them to meet my future mother-in-law. Despite my anxiety, I was happy to act as cohost as they experienced Texas for the first time. And I was grateful they were there in person, because it could have been hard to convey all of the pomp, pageantry, and personality involved in this particular celebration. In addition to Elvis, the entertainment for the evening was provided by evangelical Christian twins in their late twenties who specialize in music of the Renaissance era. Apparently, these twins had been a staple of O'Donnell family parties since they were in their teens, and they were as talented as they were eccentric. The room was a most amusing mash-up of rock 'n' roll and Renaissance. I loved it and was pleased the party went long into the big sky night.

You see, by both objective and slightly biased accounts, I was on top of the world. John and Peggy Weber's only son was engaged to the smartest, kindest, prettiest Texan sweetheart this side of the Mississippi (also *most humble*—as she strongly objects to these superlatives in my manuscript). She is a total rock and a total rock star who has the ineffable charm of Helen of Troy, or for our younger readers, Princess Anna from *Frozen*. It may be cliché to say that someone is the love of your life, but she is, and more—she is the life of my love.

In addition to planning for our upcoming nuptials, I had just finished writing a book and had a busy book tour scheduled for the next twelve months. *A Word with Weber*, my national TV show on CatholicTV, had just surpassed one hundred episodes, and I was occasionally recognized around Boston by a dedicated and wonderful fan base of female octogenarians (#IAmNotAvailableToDateYourSingle-Granddaughter). There is never a time when life is perfect, but there are occasionally times when it feels close. This point in my life was one of those times.

After the party, when the final lingering guests had gone home, I stood out by the pool looking up at the sky and had a quick check-in with God. Yes, I know God is everywhere, but after years of thinking of heaven as up and hell as down, I still tend to look up. So, as I was looking up at the stars—not shouting or whispering, but simply talking—I said, "Good night" and "Thanks, God" and "I'm really excited about this year" in a matter-of-fact way.

In retrospect, I imagine at that moment God may have chuckled.

2

Daydream Believer

As a young boy, I did not daydream about the particulars of my wedding day, but a few images had stuck in my mind of what a wedding should look like: namely, the wedding of Kermit and Miss Piggy from *The Muppets Take Manhattan*. It was in a church, all of their family (and friends from *Sesame Street*) were there, and everyone seemed happy. Strangely, I preferred the Muppet depiction of a wedding to the representation I saw in television and film, which always seemed to involve chaos.

In the show *Full House*, the character Uncle Jesse decides to jump out of an airplane the morning of his wedding. He gets stuck in a tree, descends from the tree by jumping into the bed of a truck carrying tomatoes, then steals the truck, goes to jail, and is released only when his fiancée comes to pick him up. But in the process, her car was towed, so the twosome has to hitch a ride in a bus carrying members of a gospel choir, who end up performing at their ceremony. For whatever reason, this chaos is typical. Almost every TV show depicts a wedding day as one in which the bride is running, the groom's feet are cold, or something goes wrong in the most extreme way possible (see *Game of Thrones*'s "Red Wedding").

Now, of course, I am not a talking green frog, but I have always felt a kinship with Kermit. He is a creature of simple tastes who just tries to hold the world together in whatever way he can. He has a TV show; I have a TV show. He plays the banjo; I play the guitar. He doesn't eat

frog legs; I don't either. Our voices are both a little nasal. Aside from
our color, height, and species, we're practically the same person. I'm
sure there is a deleted scene somewhere in *Muppets Take Manhattan* in
which Kermit and Miss Piggy go to Pre-Cana and discuss where and
how they want to get married, with the outcome being in a church and
by a priest. That's all I wanted too.

"I'd love to get married in Houston," Nell said as we began to discuss the where and when, once we had established the who, what,
and why. My wife grew up in Houston, a hot, sprawling city of over
two million, and the land of Beyoncé, George H.W. Bush, and BBQ,
famous for NASA and the Apollo 13 catchphrase, "Houston, we have
a problem." Once we decided on Houston, we had only a slight problem: too many choices. There are about 150 churches in the archdiocese, many of which were strong contenders for our ceremony site. We
could choose the church where my fiancée was baptized, the church
closest to her house, the prettiest church near her house, the biggest
church near her house, the church her family belonged to when she
was a kid, the modern-looking church, the church with the neon sign,
the church without the neon sign but without air conditioning, and
on and on. Ultimately, our problem was solved after a series of phone
calls, visits, availability checks, and counsel from family. We were to
be married at Holy Rosary Catholic Church, Nell's parish during her
early childhood and where she was baptized. It also happened to be a
Dominican Order parish, which was fitting, as the family friend who
would be marrying us was a Dominican priest.

And thus my simple childhood checklist of wanting to be married
in a church by a priest with loved ones surrounding us was met. I
had the perfect girl, had a church and a priest booked, and was totally
happy about anything else that would come afterward. For those of
you who haven't planned a wedding, or haven't done so in years, this
is the state of affairs: you are essentially starting a business that will

be open for two days. It involves assessment and liquidation of capital, design and creation of a website, vendor identification, cultivation of users or customers, transportation logistics, mass mailings, art design, custom photography, and approval from the board chair and CEO (i.e., your future mother-in-law and your future wife).

The choices are infinite, and everything is customizable. Would we like our mashed potatoes to be served in martini glasses at the reception? (Um, sure.) Would the save-the-date cards be 80-pound or 110-pound card stock, and would they be linen, vellum, or matte finish? (Um, Nell? What is vellum?) Would Great Aunt Millie, who's on a fixed income in California, feel pressure to give us a gift if we invited her, knowing she could not come? Or should we just send her a wedding "announcement," assuming she knows an announcement does not require sending a gift, whereas according to etiquette an invitation does? (Um, pass.) How much do you tip the cantor? Ten percent? Do you even tip the cantor if you're already paying him? Will our wedding have a hashtag? (#WebWed?)

Not all questions at this time were wedding related, though. "Matt, I just got a consultancy job to go to Rwanda the week before our wedding. Is that OK?" (*Of course, my love . . . Just please no jumping out of planes or stealing tomato trucks à la Uncle Jesse.*) And because gifts from our registry had begun to stack up in my tiny apartment and both of our leases were ending around the date of our wedding, I asked, "Should we just buy a house so we have a place to put our stuff and move in to together after the honeymoon?"

Naively treating this purchase like that of a Snickers bar, we embarked on yet another business venture: to time buying a home perfectly so that it worked for the end of both of our leases, Nell's trip to Africa, wedding decisions, mashed-potato taste testing, bachelor party planning, bachelorette weekend planning, book talks and conference presentations, and new job responsibilities at my work—all with increasingly limited intellectual, emotional, and financial capital. You might say that it was all just part of the exciting carousel that is life, moving at warp speed—with me not just reaching for the brass ring, but also for antacids and Pepto-Bismol at each turn.

In the midst of wedding planning, it was homeownership or bust. I wasn't expecting both.

3

Home Shopping Network

The first major purchase I ever made with my own money was a "big-screen," twenty-one-inch TV for $499, not including tax. The year was 2001. I was a senior in high school, and my dad had just hooked up cable in my room. I had researched TVs in the ads of the Sunday paper for weeks, scouted them out in several stores, and withdrawn enough money to splurge on the twenty-four-inch TV if I felt so inclined. That day, I walked into Circuit City a boy and left Circuit City a man.

I remember buying the TV, lugging it out to my car, and thinking I was officially an adult. I—not my dad or my mom or my sisters—owned a TV, and while afterward I was poor, I could enjoy *Walker Texas Ranger*, *Nash Bridges*, and *Murder, She Wrote* from the confines of my own room. (I had, and have, the TV-watching patterns of a sixty-year-old woman; as a result, my mother and I always have something to talk about.)

Ever since this first TV, I have treated all large purchases (anything more than $100) with great care, meticulous research, and time-consuming deliberation. Nell is the same way, if not more thorough—she is a list maker and spreadsheet keeper too. Everything is categorized and recorded digitally, and usually on paper as well. She would have been a fantastic nineteenth-century shopkeeper.

Looking at our tight calendar, we determined that we had about three to four weeks to buy a house before we would be left homeless upon returning from our honeymoon. The alternative was to rent for another year, but that wouldn't solve our storage issue or decrease our desire to never again hire movers or bribe friends and family to help us drag our stuff to another fifth-floor walk-up apartment.

Spreadsheets were made, lists compiled, and from 10 a.m. to 2 p.m. every weekend, we joined hundreds of other young couples looking for their dream home. We were like hungry hyenas scouting out the closest carcass, wondering who would get away with a home and for how much. Each weekend day, Nell carefully mapped out the optimal sequence of open houses, noting the distance from our current homes and work, the hours (most have a two- or three-hour window), proximity to each other (to avoid wasting time in transit), and appeal (Is it a neighborhood we like? Does it have a dedicated dining room?). If we were lucky, we could see a dozen homes in one shot, sometimes spending less than ten minutes inside if we knew it wasn't for us or that we had no chance of "winning" it.

Aside: It's interesting to think of winning a house, when *winning* means shelling out *all* the money you have spent your entire life saving, going into a huge amount of debt (hello, mortgage!), and making the biggest-impact decision of your life in the shortest imaginable time. Nell and I spent two wonderful, soul-searching years making sure that we were absolutely sure we wanted to spend the rest of our lives together, and then a third year as an engaged couple hammering out the details of our shared life. But when it came to buying a house, we'd give a thumbs up or down within a matter of minutes. It was crazy.

During the first week, we quickly learned that the Boston area was experiencing the "hottest" real estate market in recent history, with houses and condos selling within thirty-six to forty hours of the first open house, and for tens of thousands of dollars over the asking price. Our tail was between our legs after two straight weekends of being outbid on homes that sold for more than $100,000 over the asking price, and with all-cash offers. Cashing in my first communion money, my $25 savings bonds, and my collection of $2 bills couldn't even compete.

It wasn't looking good going into the last weekend. We had averaged seven or eight open houses per weekend (plus a record fourteen in one day), but this time, we were hoping to "Go big *and* go home."

On the night before our last night of looking, Nell and I scoured the real estate listings and shouted out addresses to input into a multiple-destination Google Map. Street names, cities, and zip codes were flying through the air like brokers' shouts on the floor of the New York Stock Exchange. Our map looked like a cartoonish maze from a children's magazine, but it made sense to us—we were going to visit as many open houses as possible in eight hours over two days and hope to God that somehow, some way, we would win a home in the last second of this game.

I will spare you the details of that weekend: much of it is just a blur, and I'd hate to inaccurately report whether I liked the second-floor porch on the corner lot better than the partially finished, funky-smelling basement near the highway. All I can tell you is that after two days, we found a townhouse next to the serpentine Mystic River, four blocks from a Catholic church, and within a one-mile radius of four movie theaters and nine pizza places. This house felt like it could be our home. In leaving the open house with my fiancée, I turned back to scout how much clearance I would have when I carried her across the threshold.

That night, we both decided to love each other "for richer and poorer" and to make an offer. We called our real estate agent and immediately biked over to the Catholic church that we hoped would be our new parish; I felt even more at home in the neighborhood. Perhaps it was a bit of divine providence, or the extra we decided to kick in above the asking price, but we found out the next day that the home would be ours. We planned to close two weeks before our wedding, one day before Nell's trip to Africa, and with just enough time to have all the boxes, furniture, and registry gifts shipped to our cozy little home.

"Let's decorate it with a river theme," I said to Nell after we closed the deal. "What is a river theme?" she asked, holding back a chuckle. It seemed to make sense to me, since we were next to a river. "Sure, darling, it can be river themed," said my future wife.

In the end, it didn't really matter that we could not do months-long research like I had for the big-screen TV from Circuit City. It was our home, and I couldn't have been more excited to share it with the woman I was about to call my wife.

4

Texas-Sized Marital Hoedown

"Chopped beef brisket on a roll, extra sauce, onions and pickles, and a side of baked potato with sour cream, cheese, butter, and green onions. Also, two slices of jalapeño cheesebread and a large lemonade, extra ice." In the shadow of a twenty-foot-tall metallic armadillo with blinking red eyes, the O'Donnell-Weber wedding weekend began. We were kicking things off at the Armadillo Palace in Houston for Mrs. O'Donnell's "Welcome to Texas" luncheon. Upon arriving, guests were treated to unlimited amounts of the best BBQ in the Houston area—a true "you are in Texas now, prepare to gain seven pounds" experience—and Texas two-step lessons from two "real" cowboys.

I was wearing cowboy boots, as were at least a half dozen of my New England relatives, who were trying to fit in and happily embrace my adopted half-Texan roots. The boot heels added at least two inches to my already-six-foot-three frame, giving me the ability to assess which of my out-of-town uncles and cousins were progressing toward baldness. As I surveyed the room, and receding hairlines, I found myself observing a living tableau of many a wedding weekend: the melding of two families into a newly forming entity. It wasn't official yet, but this was the first time I'd witnessed what I was looking forward to on our wedding day—a celebration of love with all the loved ones we could imagine in one place.

Eventually, seconds and thirds of brisket resulted in mandatory nap and lavatory time for my New England brethren, and for myself.

Virgins to both cowboy boots and the demands of the Texas two-step, we left sore but happy. It was a good warm-up for Saturday's main event.

I'll fast-forward through the Astros-Brewers game and rehearsal dinner speeches, and take you to the wedding. Showtime! That last night as a bachelor, I was sharing a hotel room with my parents in downtown Houston, but by the time I had woken up, they had already left for last-minute airport pickups, elaborate hair appointments, and providing rides to all the guests in the wedding. I had the idea that I would wake up on the morning of my wedding, go for a swim, get a hot-lather, straight-razor shave, and then golf nine holes.

Yet the reality of adding even more moving parts to the wedding day made me pass on that idea. So I planned the simplest prewedding event I could think of—no reservations, tee times, or razors. I went for a walk, on a nearly hundred-degree day. It was the kind of walk that ended up being the perfect metaphor for what I was about to embark upon; I really didn't know where my journey would lead me, but I marched happily and confidently forward, excited about the next steps I would take. In many ways, this walk was an urban pilgrimage in which I had a chance to think about how much my life would change that day—how I would coadminister a sacrament, take a formal vow, become married to another person for the rest of my life—how I would change as a result of the journey I was about to take that day. I prayed, reflected, took inventory, and dreamt, likening the experience to my own mini Camino de Santiago or hajj. I thought about how many people, in the Muslim faith in particular, change their name after making a pilgrimage, and how my future wife would too. I was a pilgrim in a foreign land, en route to a sacred place. As St. Catherine of Siena (and my mother) said, "All the way to heaven is heaven."

Now, you might assume that a groom would be nervous on the morning of his wedding. I wasn't though. I was concerned about cutting myself shaving, not about whether Nell was the right choice for me. She was. Also, our priest had asked us to memorize our vows, which, at a total of roughly twenty words, freaked me out. I am not great at remembering things, and for some reason, I was having trouble differentiating the traditional Catholic vows from the ones imprinted in my mind from the hundreds of romantic comedies I had watched over the years.

Literally, they are this simple: "I, (Matt), take you, (Nell), to be my lawful wife. To have and to hold from this day forward. For better, for worse, for richer, for poorer, in sickness and health, until death do us part."

Yet as I practiced my vows on my pilgrimage walk—a "Camino de Houston" perhaps—I kept flubbing, taking Nell to be my lawful "husband" and forgetting the order of the words. I even blanked on the first word: *I*. I hoped that in the moment the words would just naturally come to me and all would be well.

Several hours later, I stood in a tuxedo next to the altar of Holy Rosary Church. I had not cut myself shaving, the air conditioner in the church happily hummed away, and all of the people I have ever loved most in the world were under one roof.

"I, Matthew, take you, Eleanor, to be my lawful wife!" *(YES! So far so good . . .)*

"To have and to hold from this day forward." *(I knew I knew it. I was such a fool to worry that I would forget. We're in the homestretch . . .)*

And then, suddenly, my mind went blank, my mouth dry. I looked away, furrowed my brow. I was quickly descending into a spiral of nervousness and terror. I had no idea what came next! How long had I stopped talking for? I was angry at the priest: *WHY DID THIS HAVE TO BE MEMORIZED?! Oh, crap, I'm glad we didn't spring for the wedding videographer. Oh, God help me.* I looked into the eyes of my almost wife to try to see how she was feeling. *Is she mad? Does she think I got cold feet at the last possible moment? Oh God, help me . . .*

The beauty of the sacrament of marriage is that it is the only sacrament in the Catholic Church that does not need to be administered by an ordained minister. The sacrament is sealed by the couple through the power and grace of God. During our Pre-Cana study, the priest told us that he didn't even really need to be there for the sacramental part; that the marriage was between us and God.

So while I found myself quickly asking God to help me remember my poorly memorized vows, my partner in God's love was looking right at me with bright, soothing eyes and a reassuring smile.

"For better, for worse," Nell mouthed ever so subtly as my brain and mouth recalibrated. It is poetic and beautiful that her first act of being my wife was helping me get better from worse. She was the answer to my prayers to God.

"For better, for worse, for richer, for poorer, in sickness and health, until death do us part," I said. *(BOOYA! HOORAY! I am the happiest forgetful idiot in the world!)* Unsurprisingly, Nell perfectly elocuted her vows, and we were hitched. I know everyone likes to hear about the reception, the food, the dancing, the cake, the colors, the music, the magic. But for me, the best moment of my wedding day was that very first moment of my marriage, feeling profound love when my wife kindly helped me in a time of need. As the night closed and the final song played—"Sweet Caroline," in honor of my mother and all her fellow rabid Red Sox fans—our plan was to sprint out of the reception area as our guests blew bubbles at us, a suggestion of the photographer, much to the chagrin of the powerful rice lobby, I'm sure.

And so we grabbed hands and ran through a shower of bubbles blown from the lips of our loved ones. Once clear of this welcomed barrage, we looked back and realized we had no plan. The "bubble run" was the last wedding event on the checklist. We somehow had forgotten to plan what would happen between leaving the reception hall and arriving at our hotel room that night. We had already left in the grandest of ways and couldn't bear to return through the same line of people for an awkward second good-bye and a "Can someone give us a ride?"

And so, arm in arm, under a bright midnight moon, wearing our fanciest clothes and now together in the best of ways, we just kept walking. Our hotel wasn't far away, and we were always up for a new adventure. It would be my second walk through Houston that day; this one I much preferred. It was much cooler, and I was in the greatest of company.

5

What Happened on Our Wedding Night in the Honeymoon Suite

The wedding night, the honeymoon suite—no, I'm not talking about those details! In fact, my wife would absolutely kill me if I even went into any specifics about our kiss during the ceremony. "Matty, I'm glad it's over," she said as we made it to the hotel that night. "And I'm also glad it's just beginning."

The front lobby of the chic Hotel ZaZa was packed with people. We were a bit surprised that there were two other grooms and two other brides there, reminding us that while we were the most special people of the evening in our minds, our distinction was shared—and that certain things in life do turn back into a pumpkin at the end of the night. As was the case for me on most evenings with an odd eating schedule, I felt queasy and thought a late-night sandwich would help. We called room service and plopped down on our plush pillow-top bed. While waiting for our food, we strangely ended up watching *The Lawrence Welk Show* on PBS, and for much longer than we might have thought would be the case on our wedding night. There was something strangely comforting about this variety show—its format, the singers, and the fact that we weren't responsible for their travel logistics.

Our room service eventually arrived, and we picked at our food like snobby birds pecking around generic birdseed. We then turned into bed, but my stomach was still churning and feeling off. This wasn't the first time I had gone to bed with a sour stomach; antacids, various other remedies, and sleep usually helped to calm the subtle but persistent pain in my lower belly. On this night, of all nights, I was hoping for some gastrointestinal peace, but I would not be so lucky.

It seemed that the martini-glassed mashed potatoes, cheese tortellini, roasted chicken, and two Shirley Temples wanted to make a reverse journey just as my new wife and I were falling asleep. In the nick of time, I was able to navigate past the rental tux, the sleepy bride, and her pristine white dress to find the hotel ice bucket, which would become my new friend for the next two minutes. I was hoping my wife would think this was a bad dream and not have it be the memory of her first night with her new husband—a tired, gangly husband in boxer shorts, with his head in a bucket, waking her up with unpleasant sights, sounds, and smells. In fact, it was the smell I was most worried about, so I put the bucket on the room service tray and placed it outside the door.

"Matt, you really might want to warn the hotel staff about what you just introduced to a public hallway," Nell said in a half-asleep yet fully rational state. Already the sage wisdom and counsel of my wife was in full effect, making me a better person and improving the world.

"Right," I said, and then picked up the phone and dialed 0. That night I fell asleep next to my new wife in a honeymoon suite that smelled of rotten tortellini. Yet fragrance-free love permeated the air that evening, as I was officially, formally, and in the eyes of God and man, tethered to my best friend. Someone who cared about the employee in the hallway finding surprise "ice." Someone who found forty-five minutes of *The Lawrence Welk Show* the perfect entertainment for a new couple after eighteen hours of being "on." Someone who, while already fast asleep, instinctually hugged me back after I cozied up next to her in bed, finally, ready to sleep.

It was not the typical wedding night "excitement" that I had anticipated; rather, it was an unceremonious nightcap at the end of an already-packed day that showcased the first of many signposts of love that one finds as a newlywed.

6

And the Beat Goes On

The sign outside the volcano read: "If you are in need of medical assistance or if the volcano erupts, please calmly exit your cabin and walk down the gravel road to the bell. Ring the bell and wait for the helicopter to come and rescue you."

It continued: "What is the status of the volcano?

Arenal Volcano, which lay dormant for centuries, erupted in 1968 and has been active, but in the last months the Arenal Volcano is in a passive phase with very little activity as a part of its natural evolution."

And finally:

"Is Arenal Observatory Lodge & Spa a safe place?

Arenal Observatory Lodge & Spa is situated on a ridge 120 meters above Lake Arenal, southeast of this active La Fortuna volcano. The ridge rises between the Agua Caliente and Quebrada Danta rivers. This topographical feature is important as it keeps lava flows from affecting the Arenal lodge. The lodge is within Zone 'D' (Low Danger Area) near Volcáno Arenal. Moreover, as prevailing winds are from the east, the Arenal Volcano lodge would seldom be affected by ash or other fallout from a major eruption."

This is where we spent our honeymoon, in the shadow of a Costa Rican volcano that was rumbling and churning, perhaps ready to burst at any moment.

Note to high school English students: the previous sentence is the definition of narrative foreshadowing. Continue reading.

From whitewater rafting and hot-stone massages to thermal-pool dipping and mile-long zip-lining, our Costa Rican honeymoon was one of the most exciting weeks of my life. We were carefree kids, and life in Costa Rica came as advertised—*pura vida*, "pure living." To non-honeymooners, we may have been annoying with our constant handholding and lovey-dovey sitting on the same side of the booth at restaurants. Yes, we were "those people," but we had a good excuse, and we were prepared to show our wedding certificate and still-shiny rings to the disgusted eye rollers.

Whether we were hanging hundreds of feet over a cloud-shrouded rain forest, or just sitting in the hotel and waiting out a rainstorm by watching episodes of *The Wire*, life was grand. Even outside the wonder of the week, we were both feeling good. Nell had just gotten into a prestigious doctoral program at Harvard and would continue consulting for the rest of the summer. I would be returning home to a great position at Harvard while continuing my book tour on the weekends, bringing me to colleges, conferences, and parishes across the country. I also would be appearing in a new CBS News documentary called *What's So Funny about Religion?*, and a local school had just asked to use my book as part of its religion and theology curriculum.

On our honeymoon, we made a pact not to check e-mails or worry about calendars. In fact, I even created my first ever out-of-the-office e-mail that included this message: "In Costa Rica, we expect more zip line than online."

"Have you checked e-mails yet?" Nell asked, about four days into the trip.

"No, did you? And maybe do you want to?" I asked.

We grabbed mugs of hot tea and cozy seats next to the floor-to-ceiling windows looking out over the volcano, and plugged back in. I'm sure the hummingbirds, sloths, and howler monkeys all shed a simultaneous tear that moment, mourning the loss of yet another couple who had chosen to spend time online. We felt somewhat guilty about breaking our deal, but not totally chagrined that the reality we were about to revisit wasn't one we sought permanent escape from. We loved our lives, our visit to Costa Rica, and the fact that 226 people had "liked" our Facebook status change to newly married.

Little did I know, though, that my stomach was about to unfriend the rest of my body.

7

Completing the Dream

As a child growing up in the quarry-and-farm town of East Long-meadow, Massachusetts, I always asked Santa for three things: a pond, a dog, and a batting cage.

I was typically on the "nice list" (despite routine lapses when I had harassed one of my sisters or had a mean thought about the opposing Little League team's pitcher), and I was lucky enough that Santa seemed to consistently reward my struggle to be good with Nerf guns and cash, not clothes. He knew I hated clothes because I often wrote "not clothes" in my early letters to him. I knew my "big three" list was a bit of a reach, but I had seen enough TV Christmas specials to believe that anything was possible on Christmas morning.

Knowing my parents were trained and certified North Pole elves who assisted Santa with many of these presents, I would often gauge their reactions when discussing my list. "Where do you buy a pond?" I would ask my parents, who knew I had limited knowledge of Frederick Law Olmsted and his landscape architecture at my young age.

"Why do you think you'll be the only one taking care of the dog?" I would whine, always the follow-up to my mother's prediction that a new puppy would be a furrier fourth child for her to feed and clean. "Wait until you're a grown-up," she would say.

"Are batting cages expensive?" I'd wonder, not really knowing exactly what went into the construction, maintenance, and logistics of an actual backyard batting cage. (In the end, I really did want for nothing. Everything I needed, I got, and most everything I wanted, I also got. I think my parents walked that fine line of making me feel special yet not spoiling me, hoping their kid wouldn't grow up an entitled brat, like Veruca Salt from *Charlie and the Chocolate Factory*.)

And so Christmas came and went, and each year I received wonderful gifts, but none that barked, and none that needed inordinate amounts of weatherproof wrapping paper. I started to wonder whether my dreams were too big, my wants too much, the capacity of the gift-giving elf employer too tapped.

And then came the Christmas of 1995. I knew something was up, as part of our house was "off-limits" on Christmas morning.

We have some strange Christmas traditions in the Weber household. First, we all march down the stairs, hands on each other's backs, chanting, "Follow D to the tree!" ("D" being Dad, leading his eager family to their haul.) However, before we get to the tree, the Weber train stops at the crèche set and sings "Happy Birthday" to Jesus. Then, the family train uncouples and we storm the family room like ants on a discarded piece of watermelon at a picnic.

This year, though, there seemed to be fewer presents, which had been neatly placed in piles around the room. In the "shared presents" quadrant of the family room lay a few large boxes. Typically, this is where the big-ticket items were supposed to be—the twenty-one-inch TVs, combo BETA/VHS tape players, and passes to Disney World. I had a good feeling about this year.

I opened my presents the way I ate my dinner, rushing through the salad, bread, entrée, and veggies to get to the dessert. The shared presents ended up being part of an elaborate scavenger hunt around the house, with clues on the refrigerator and in the bathroom. We finally ended up in part of the house that had been "off-limits." I was sure it was a dog the whole time, the cute cuddly one I had pleaded with

Santa for, and I was already in love with him for being so quiet and calm as we opened our appetizer and entrée presents.

So as we turned the corner, there it was—a batting cage. Well, at least the giant pitching machine that would be the centerpiece of the one-thousand-square-foot, fully netted area that would soon take up 25 percent of our backyard. Some kids had pools; we had a batting cage. My bighearted father, with some input and advice from Santa, had built us a batting cage with all the bells and whistles, complete with an MLB-approved home plate, batting helmets, hitting tees, and all the trimmings. It was the best present a baseball-loving young American like me could have ever asked for. And yet, for just a moment, I still mourned that it wasn't a dog.

Fifteen years later, my new wife and I got off the plane from Costa Rica. We took a cab to our new home and proceeded to sit in the one chair and on the one rug we had previously moved in to our townhouse. Since we are both goal makers and list keepers, we made a checklist:

Marriage. Check.

House. Check.

Job/School. Check.

"Can I add one more thing to that list?" I asked.

"Sure, sweetie. Is it another chair? Because we definitely need a second one," she said, sitting on the one chair.

"I'd like to get a dog."

I was a few months away from turning thirty, living in my first place that allowed pets, and I was married to someone who could help me feed, walk, and clean up after a pup. She smiled and nodded yes.

We adopted a seven-pound Australian terrier mix from the Animal Rescue League of Boston later that week. We named him "Duck." And Duck actually likes to run around the still-intact, recently refurbished batting cage in my parents' backyard. Life was more than good. It was grand.

However, I am still in the market for a good place to buy a pond.

8

Shit Hits Fan (Can I Write That in a Catholic Book?)

Most stomachaches tend to go away. Something gives—a virus or a bug—and then you move on with life. Oftentimes we'll consume Tums or Maalox and lots of water, and close proximity to a toilet is requisite. This is normal.

What isn't normal is lying down in the aisle of a grocery store, telling your wife that you may need to see a doctor, and subsequently checking yourself into the Harvard infirmary for the day because you're leaking out the posterior. What isn't normal is going to bed every night knowing that whatever you ate or tried to eat that day will not stay down, and that you will soon be reliving a home version of your unsexy wedding night, sans dress hurtling and ice-bucket assistance. What isn't normal is seeing multiple doctors and having them all think something is amiss, but being unable to prescribe you something that will actually help. What isn't normal is stepping on a scale and realizing you have accidentally lost thirty pounds in the course of a few months without even noticing.

I had lived a blessed life for almost thirty years. I had never gotten sick—in fact, I had perfect attendance from kindergarten through twelfth grade, one of only two students to be recognized for this epic marathon of healthiness. I took pride in being tough and resilient whenever any minor health issue came up. Yet inexplicably, I couldn't lick what seemed like a permanent stomachache that had me always feeling nauseous, or as my wife would say, "feeling puny."

As a distraction from this prolonged malady, my wife surprised me with a trip to Ireland for my thirtieth birthday in October. We are both of Irish descent, but neither of us had visited the old sod, and we were looking forward to a restful break and hopefully some European relief from my tummy troubles. The itinerary was actually very similar to my parents' honeymoon, about thirty-five years earlier: we'd fly into Dublin and take a left-side-of-the-road sojourn around the Ring of Kerry, stopping at castles and charming villages along the way.

Leading up to the trip, I could see the pain and concern in my wife's eyes every time I returned to bed after my nightly emesis. "Matty, I'm worried about you. I'm glad we have an endoscopy scheduled for you on Friday," she said calmly.

For those of you who aren't doctors or haven't dealt with such issues, an endoscopy is when a doctor sticks a fancy, snakelike camera down your esophagus and investigates what is happening in your stomach. It is affectionately referred to as a "colonoscopy of the throat." I was really hoping this new home movie would shed some light on the pain and nip it in the bud once and for all.

In the meantime, the days seemed to drag. I was eating very little but still going to work. I would close my door and lie down in my office, finding some relief for my stomach as I lay outstretched, but I could stay there only for brief stints, since I had an inordinate fear that a coworker would walk by and think I was sleeping on the job or lying dead in my office. Neither option was preferable, and yet I still trudged through the week.

On Thursday, the day before my endoscopy, I had a morning meeting and found I could not keep my head up. I could speak, hear, and listen, but my body would not let me stay upright. I'm very comfortable with my coworkers (and at the time was also very desperate), so I asked them if I could put my head down on the conference table and continue to participate from that position. For the next thirty minutes, I gave my reports and feedback on their projects as a crumpled heap of a man, barely enunciating, looking like a kindergartener told to put his head on his desk in a time-out. No food, no relief, just one more day until this would all be straightened out. I was sure of it—after all, I've got a small wooden plaque that says "12 Years of Perfect Attendance" to prove just how committed I am to not being sick.

Unbeknownst to me, my wife received an e-mail shortly after the meeting from Lory, one of my dear friends at the office (in addition to my boss, Mike Rodman, also a dear friend, I was fortunate to have people looking out for me all hours of the day):

> *FYI, Matt will probably kill me for sending this e-mail, but I just wanted you to know that he looks rough. We were just in a meeting and he was really dragging. I told him to go home and take a nap with the dog! I suspect he won't, so I just wanted to give you a heads up. :(*

Nell responded:

> *Hi Lory,*
>
> *Thanks for e-mailing. Matt is really lucky to have such caring coworkers.*
>
> *I'm taking him home now. Right before that meeting we met with the doctor at urgent care to see if there was something that could be done to make him feel better. He's been dealing with some really bad stomach issues for a while, and it has been especially bad this week.*
>
> *Do you mind looping Mike in as well?*
>
> *Thanks again for e-mailing and for keeping an eye on my special guy.*

The next morning, my wife drove me to Kenmore Square in Boston for my appointment. "I just heard back from the bed-and-breakfast owner in Dingle. We're all set for next week—he sounds so charming," Nell said.

She read me the first words of his e-mail: "Good evening, Eleanor, and greetings from this most special part of Ireland. Many thanks for your decision to stay with us at Pax House."

I adored this idea: getting better that day, then flying over to a house of peace in the most special part of Ireland. It sounded like a plan to me! Upbeat but anxious, I went through all the normal steps of preprocedure care and was injected with a special cocktail that would make me "float away" as a camera slid down my throat. I've never done drugs, so when they're mandatory for hospital procedures, I'm always curious to see where my brain will take me. I was hoping to escape to Ireland in my mind during this legal drug experience, perhaps checking in to Dingle and reporting back to Nell on my return.

Upon waking up, optimism about the future immediately shifted to pessimism when I saw the looks on the faces around me.

"You need to go to the emergency room right now," I was informed by both my doctor and my wife. Apparently, the tiny camera could not see anything in my stomach, as it was nearly swollen shut. Lucky for me, a world-class teaching hospital was just down the street, so my wife grabbed the car, picked me up by the side of the road, drove a few blocks over, and walked me into the ER.

Still woozy, I really . . . didn't . . . know . . . what . . . was . . . happening. It sucked. I checked in with the reception and then did what most people do in ERs—I waited. To the naked eye, I looked completely healthy. And if you asked my symptoms, it was "my tummy hurts," which won't move you along in the world of hospital triage.

For the first two hours in the waiting room, Nell and I made phone calls and coached each other through higher and higher levels of stupid iPhone games. During the second two hours, we spent time counting our blessings, especially the fact that we hadn't had to spend all that much time in emergency rooms over the course of our lives. These places are necessary and sad and stressful—and yet strangely competitive. Everyone who comes in wants to be seen ASAP. The word *emergency* comes from the Latin *emergere*, meaning "arise, bring to light," which is exactly what each person wanted.

Around the fifth hour, I started to wonder whether that day was a particularly clumsy day in Boston or whether I was just unlucky. I longed for things to be like the deli counter, where your number is picked and you are helped. Yet I respected the calculus of triage, from the French *trier*, meaning to "pick out." I just knew I was going to be last picked, and by hour six, I was at peace with that.

Finally, I was moved from the waiting room to the interior hallway, where I was prepped, poked, IVed, and questioned. It wasn't terribly clear what I was being prepped for, but I was placed on a gurney and in a gown, and it seemed each new medical expert coming by had a new round of overlapping questions.

"Matt, we don't know how much longer it will be until they are able to get someone to see you for long enough to figure out what's going on," said Nell.

We had not expected to be away from home so long. "I want to be able to stay in touch with our families, who are going to go crazy if they don't get regular updates about your status. Our phones are going to die and I need to drop the dog off at a friend's house since we might be here all night. Will you be OK if I run home to get our chargers and take care of Duck?" asked Nell. "I'll be gone less than forty minutes, I promise! See you soon and I love you."

I kissed Nell good-bye and tried to come up with a new way to entertain myself for yet another hour. More sitting, more waiting, all alone in the corner nook of a very busy Boston emergency room. And then it happened: a feeling I had never felt before was registering in my brain as *Huh, this is different* and then, *Um—ow—what is this?*

It was the strangest, most acute sensation I've ever felt—like someone had spilled a bowl of lava in my abdominal region, with its contents slowly making their way up my body cavity, creeping toward my heart and lungs. When I skin my knee, I go "Ouch." When I twist my ankle, I say "Ahh." When it felt like slow lava was burning a trail north through my innards, I yelled, "Help! Help!"

At first, one nurse came over to ask what was wrong.

"Something is happening. Something is happening in my stomach."

I was a communications professional at Harvard, and the best I could do was use the words *something* and *happening* to describe the something that was happening.

"There is a burning inside me, or I'm allergic to some medicine you gave me. Something is wrong." I was yelling and writhing, trying to contort my body in a way that would guide this mysterious, hot stomach juice away from critical organs.

"Help, someone help me!" I was shrieking like a crazy person. I could see it in the furrowed brows of the nurses who came over to play with my IV and check my chart.

The "something" was still creeping up my body, and all I kept thinking was that whatever it was—a burst internal pipe, an allergic reaction to medicine, some weird endoparasitoid extraterrestrial species from the movie *Alien*—I couldn't let it reach my heart. I was an American Studies major and film minor in college. I have two master's degrees and a business certificate, but my knowledge of human anatomy comes mostly from the board game Operation. I didn't know what was going on, but I was starting to feel like someone was playing with my insides. Lights started flashing and buzzers were ringing; alarms went off, machines screamed, and suddenly a muted rainbow of individuals in medical scrubs, lab coats, and nurse's uniforms appeared in front of me, all of them looking confused.

Why in the world was this seemingly healthy guy with a stomachache now registering a heart rate of over 170? I wondered the same thing as my hospital "wearable" let me know that my heart was not just racing, but sprinting like I'd never felt before.

"Someone help me, please! It's burning!"

The heart-rate monitor kept chirping higher and higher, and the slow slithering of the warm sensation inside me moved closer and closer. I began to wonder whether this was how it would end for me.

During moments when you really, truly think you are going to die, it's interesting what goes through your head. Certainly there's confusion, clearly there's pain, but for me, there was not much else but a determination and focus to *not die*. I didn't pray for help or look back on my life, feeling ready to move on. I locked into total survival mode, moved into a fetal position, and focused on staying alert, awake.

Doctors and nurses were injecting things into my IV, conferring, adjusting, and evaluating the situation. I glanced up and could see someone cutting through the crowd, making his way to the front of the group; he looked exactly like what a casting agent would call "Confident Surgeon No. 1" in a hospital drama. It was clear he was in charge, and likely the best person to answer what I thought might've been my final question.

"Am I going to die?" I squeaked out as my fingers clenched and I could hear, feel, and see my heartbeat hit new highs.

"No!" he said, in a tone that was both authoritative and seemed to indicate that the question was insulting to him.

I had experienced this uniquely effective tone before, having been a student in Catholic schools for twenty years of my life: "you're in trouble with the nuns, so you better behave and do what they say or you'll be in even more trouble." It was a tone I had been conditioned to both fear and obey wholeheartedly as I was carefully cultivated in the strict education of the Sisters of St. Joseph. It was a tone I did not dispute or question, but quickly obeyed.

All of a sudden, something changed. Something stopped.

I don't know if it was the collective choir of the Sisters of St. Joseph summoned through the doctor's "No!" that seemed to quell this fire, or if it was the massive amount of sedative that managed to de-escalate the situation at the same time. I like to think it was a little of both, but the heart-rate monitor slowed, the burning "something" came to a stop, and I was whisked away into a giant cylindrical machine to snag some new pictures of my stomach and determine exactly what had just happened.

Walking briskly back in with two phone chargers, Nell was approached by hospital personnel, who let her know why her husband was not where she had left him.

9

Gut Check

The year was 1885. A young Italian physician, Eugenio Casati, was traveling on a scientific tour of Europe and found himself in the operating theater of the Second Surgical Clinic of the University of Vienna. Looking on, he would observe and later report on the first procedure for the surgical removal of part or all of the stomach. It would later be known as Bilroth II, named after the Austrian surgeon and amateur musician Theodor Bilroth, who was performing the surgery and is today considered the founding father of modern abdominal surgery.

For the hundreds of stomach surgeons reading this book, maybe you know that this was a popular surgery in the late 1800s. It has since become much less relevant with the advent of proton-pump inhibitors and nonsurgical treatments that reduce gastric acid production (i.e., Prilosec and Omeprazole). Almost 120 years later, though, and four thousand miles from Vienna, this same surgery was about to be performed.

A quick CT scan of my abdomen showed that my stomach had perforated and was spilling stomach acid (i.e., lava) into the rest of my body cavity. My stomach was nearly swollen shut, which explained why I hadn't been able to keep any food down. It was also surprisingly filled with unhealed, scarred ulcers, and it was much larger than it should have been (probably because it was swelling and stretching as I kept eating despite inflammation caused by ulcers). Essentially, my stomach was leaking and enormous!

After the scan, after they hurriedly told me and Nell that I would have emergency surgery later that very night, as soon as an operating room was available, the surgeon stopped by to prepare us for what was to come. He explained that I had a hole in my stomach, and while this was very serious, not to worry. He'd be able to "patch it right up," and I'd likely be back in the recovery room in less than two hours. Unfortunately, things didn't go as planned.

When the team of surgeons cut into me and saw the mess I had left them, they determined that instead of just patching over the hole in my stomach, they would have to do something much more drastic: the Bilroth II. But there was one problem: my lead surgeon knew the surgery existed but had never seen one performed, let alone performed one himself. As I said, it was an old surgery that was done not very often, so it wasn't part of the typical repertoire of surgeons younger than fifty (it'd be like tweeting millennials grappling with a typewriter).

Lucky for me, my surgeon was able to call in an old-timer who, with the help of the rest of the team, was able to snip, cut, reroute some tubes, and put me back together. Theodor Bilroth would've been proud.

Originally planned to be a two-hour surgery, it took nearly six hours. They ended up removing the lower 30 percent of my stomach and creating a whole new path for how food is moved and processed through my gastrointestinal tract.

Of course, in that moment, I knew nothing about nineteenth-century surgeons or late-night calls to mentors. I knew nothing about two hours becoming six, or what was or was not removed from inside of me.

I woke up in a room that felt white, very white, with three women standing over my bed, soothing me in dulcet tones. One was a nurse, the other two were my wife and mother.

"Hello, darling, how are you feeling? You just went through a pretty big surgery," Nell said.

Concern dripped from everyone's face. Before I asked for a much-needed recap of the past several hours, I knew my loved ones needed a smile.

"Please tell me they didn't remove my penis. *I need it*," I whispered, winking at my wife.

I'm really not sure whether that was an appropriate thing to say in front of my mother, my embarrassed wife, and a stranger, but at least for a second, we had a laugh, and I could always blame the drugs later for the comment. I suppose it's also hard to get too mad at a guy who just got out of surgery.

"You still have your penis," said my mother, gingerly uttering a sentence I never thought I'd hear my mother say.

I took a quick survey of my body to see exactly what had changed. For one, there were at least two dozen staples going down my body in a precise line, starting near my sternum and ending at my belly button. There was a tube coming out of my nose and at least a few coming out from under my gown. There was another tube coming out of my abdomen, leading to a small bag full of black liquid that was slowly draining out of me. I looked like a beached cyborg octopus and likely had the mental capacity of one as well.

I was soon filled in by a series of doctors, surgeons, nurses, and family members as to what had happened. Artist renderings of my new stomach were drawn on white notepads, and words like *duodenum* and *jejunum* were introduced to my vocabulary. While pushed along in a surprisingly comfy bed, I was informed I'd spend an indefinite amount of time in the acute-care recovery wing on the fourth floor, the same wing that had treated the victims of the Boston Marathon bombing less than a year earlier.

After the haze of the first day had passed and the reality of what had happened sunk in, my goal was to get better and to get out as soon as possible. Of course some housekeeping had to be done—it's hard to be in the middle of a book tour and a full-time job at Harvard and then suddenly fall off the face of the earth. I had asked my wife to reschedule a book talk I had planned for that weekend.

Unfortunately, in my drug-induced and weakened state, I didn't give her many details, just that it was at St. Cecilia's Parish. Nell knew that the talk was local, but she quickly learned that in the Boston area, where the most concentrated population of American Catholics live, there is a St. Cecilia's in nearly every town. I didn't know this at the time, but apparently she had some lovely conversations with some very kind and concerned pastoral secretaries at St. So-and-So's of Boston, Leominster, and Concord.

I also notified my boss, Mike Rodman, as to what had happened and why I wouldn't be at work the following day(s). He visited me the very next day, told me he'd personally take over all of my job responsibilities in my absence, and, knowing humor can be the best medicine, sent me the board game Operation as a get-well gift. Several other colleagues also visited me, but I was paranoid that the broader community message would be "Matt is out of work for who-knows-how-long because of his stomachache." So, I did something really stupid. In an attempt to get ahead of the "story," I idiotically posted a selfie of my stapled stomach on Facebook and Instagram, and provided everyone with a brief synopsis of what was going on (I thought about blaming this on the drugs too, but I knew what I was doing). I even labored over which Instagram filter to use to make my stomach look less gross and better lit. Again, for a communications professional, it was a total bonehead move—and I would later find out from family and friends that it was the definition of "graphic oversharing" and TMI.

Day two involved some goal setting: "Matt, I'm going to need you to do one thing for me today. Your goal today is to pass gas," one of the nurses said. Apparently farting would be a step in the right direction toward ensuring that my new plumbing was in working order. Little did the nurse know that I come from a long line of Weber men who are particularly talented at this kind of thing; not only are we prolific in the art of flatulence, but the scent of our emissions is rather pungent too.

"No problem," I said, thinking that what I once could do so easily I could still do now. If all they needed was a fart today, it would be a breeze (pun intended). Yet anyone who has gone through a major medical procedure knows that not all things that you used to be able to do come so easily afterward. For starters, I found myself unable to move my upper body, because the stomach muscles of my core had been severed in order to get underneath. Moving my upper body seemed like a bigger, longer-term goal. If all they needed was a fart today, by comparison, it should be a piece of cake.

Since meeting my wife and realizing she had joined the club of Weber women who do not particularly appreciate our "brand," I found it ironic that something I had tried to avoid doing in her presence was now the only thing I was supposed to be doing in her presence.

"Don't worry about a thing. I've already decided to take at least this week off from school, Matty. I've written to my professors and let them know I need to be here with you," she said. This would be tough on her. She was just a few weeks into starting a new doctoral program and was already living out our vows, "in sickness and in health." When she said them, she had no idea how soon she would draw on them, but I felt my love for her grow deeper, just by having her next to me in my time of need.

"I think I've got one coming," I said to her. "But I can't really tell if anything is coming out." In what I believe could be grounds for sainthood, my wife walked over, pulled up my blanket, put her head close to my rear end, and sniffed.

"Sorry, Matt. False alarm," she said.

This unholy ritual would go on for seven more hours, with intermittent starts, sniffs, and stops. Looking to resolve this Sisyphean task, I resorted to coaching. First I asked Google, "How to force farting?" and subsequently, as the sun was setting on my daily goal, I even asked the nurse if she knew of any way to help me fart.

As visiting time was about to end, I gave it one last try.

"I think I did it. I think I farted, Nell!" I said with the enthusiasm of a guy who had just split the atom.

And so, for the umpteenth time that day, my classy, proper, well-mannered Texan wife got up from her chair, pulled up my blanket, stuck her head next to my butt, and took in a big whiff.

Her head quickly retreated from underneath the covers; it could mean only one thing.

"Oooh, gross. Definitely a fart."

Her agony was my ecstasy! I had finally farted!

Looking back on those first two days in the hospital, everything had been pretty crappy: I had offended my 1,310 Facebook friends with stomach-staple nudity, I was being tested for various forms of stomach cancer, and I continued to concern my wife and parents with my recovery and health scare. I was trying not to think about why all of this had happened to me.

While I still couldn't move my upper body, I sure could move gas through my bowels, and I was pretty lucky to be married to the kind of woman who was willing to sacrifice her olfactory integrity to confirm twenty-third-hour flatulence. I looked up at my wife and saw my wedding ring dangling from a necklace. Having weighed 205 pounds before my wedding, I was now at 155. Apparently, my fingers had gotten so thin that the wedding ring we had just exchanged a few months earlier was sliding off.

So she was wearing both rings—hers on her hand and mine near her heart—and I took comfort in knowing the depths of her love and the calm as she tried to hold us and our new marriage together. "In sickness and in health . . ."

And during every hour of visiting time, I felt a strength from her that kept me sane. For the first few days, the nurses didn't even force her to leave overnight. I think they knew that she needed to be with me and I needed to be with her. When they finally started enforcing the rules and I had become more stable, she'd leave as late as possible, staying even after visiting hours ended at 10 p.m. And that is when things got really interesting . . .

10

Hail Mary, Full of Something . . .

From the age of five to fifteen, I had a recurring dream: a three-foot-tall Lego clown at the bottom of my childhood home's staircase would suddenly come alive, chase me up the steps, snicker an evil laugh, and then stab me with a knife. Afraid of clowns for most of my childhood, I was terrified when my father brought home a giant model of a happy, yellow clown sitting in a car, holding his hand up in a Princess Diana wave. I had the great fortune of growing up with a dad who actually worked for the Lego company, and it was not unusual for him to "bring home his work" from time to time. Most days it was a simple kit; my favorite was the monorail, but the pirate ship was also a big family favorite. Occasionally, the Lego model shop would sell outdated or used floor models to employees, and my father loved to surprise us. The first surprise gift was a giant Lego chess set; the second, a pair of pilgrims standing next to each other, looking very historical and happy; the third, the waving clown.

For some reason, the clown was placed right at the foot of the stairs in the front hallway so it was the first thing we saw when we entered the house or came downstairs. Often, I would be the last one up at night and my mother would scream, "Make sure to shut off the lights!"

The problem with it being nighttime, and with the task of shutting off all the downstairs lights, is that there would be up to five seconds spent in total darkness with the smiling, probably definitely evil clown from my bad dreams guarding the way upstairs like Cerberus, the three-headed guard dog of Hades.

Nighttime was always a stressful time for me. As for many children, once it got dark and quiet, I would go from basking in the warm glow of my loving family to feeling alone, scared, and vulnerable. My daily routine of flipping off all the switches and sprinting past the Lego clown always ended with me out of breath but relieved. In addition to speed, the Holy Spirit helped me get through this time. I had always been a fan of the Holy Spirit, and I felt a special kinship to this one-third of the Holy Trinity. We had a unique relationship, different from mine with God and with Jesus, both of whom I had always imagined as people (of course). The Holy Spirit, however, was an all-purpose quiet grace that could provide unspoken protection and peace when I needed it.

While the initial sprints past that clown at night were harrowing, I eventually saw this nightly ritual as an opportunity to team up with the Holy Spirit to get over my fear. And while I still felt afraid of that clown, I was less afraid knowing that the Holy Spirit was with me. Whatever form the Spirit takes, I've always been comforted by its presence, and to this day, I attribute that weird, creepy clown to my close relationship with the Holy Spirit.

At a hospital, though, there is never a true nighttime. With hourly vitals checks and continual chart readings, it's hard to get into a restful groove, let alone a full sleep cycle. I had a ninety-year-old roommate whose medical needs seemed worse than mine, and so for the two of us, while the sun set and the moon rose each night, there was little difference in the pace of things at any given hour.

It had likely been forty-eight hours since I had last *really* slept (not counting drug-laced dozing), and there seemed to be a temporary calm in activity on the third evening. My roommate was snoring, the machines were quiet, and no one was around. It was just me, alone with my thoughts and left to my own devices. I had been told shortly after surgery that the more pain killers I took, the longer the recovery time would be, so I had stopped pressing my wonderful morphine button and had refused even milder pain pills that day. For the first time since being admitted, I was completely lucid. I looked around the room, read the brands of all of the devices that surrounded me, and glanced at the clock.

It was 3 a.m. I was not in charge of shutting off the lights before heading up to bed. There was no staircase or menacing clown in a tiny car. It was late and dark, and I was scared. Typically, this is when I would've connected with my old friend the Holy Spirit to ask for some assistance in falling asleep or finding peace. As I lay there thinking about the Holy Spirit, I realized I really hadn't prayed to God at night, thought once about Jesus, or connected in a spiritual way while recovering in the hospital. This clear realization surprised me; I usually connect with God in all sorts of ways during times of need. I thought back to when I thought I was dying in the ER, and I was perplexed that in that moment, I wasn't praying—praying hadn't even crossed my mind. I had been in total survival mode and, upon reflection, I wondered why prayer wasn't connected to my survival in that moment.

Regardless of what had happened in the ER, I was awake, aware, and ready to open myself up to God in a time of great need for the first time since I almost met him at the pearly gates. I figured a simple Hail Mary was a good starter to any spiritual session, so I began a quiet recitation: "Hail Mary, full of grace, the Lord is with thee. Blessed . . ." I stopped. I didn't want to stop but I had to. I started again.

"Hail Mary, full of grace, the Lord is with thee. Blessed . . ." I stopped again. What was happening?

"Hail Mary, full of grace, the Lord is with thee. Blessed . . ." Again, I paused.

I couldn't remember the rest of the Hail Mary.

A prayer I had said tens of thousands of times in that moment I could not finish. I couldn't *pray* that evening, and that was one of the scariest moments of my life. When all else had failed at other times, I always had prayer—in moments of ecstasy and of agony, times of celebration and hopeless causes—prayer had been there for me, until that night.

I looked down at my stomach and counted and recounted the staples. I shifted positions ever so slightly. I readjusted one of the four tubes protruding from my body. If I was really uncomfortable, I could have taken a pain killer or called a nurse. But there is no button to push in a fancy hospital bed that can help you pray, and I wasn't going to ask a nurse to fill me in on the second part of the Hail Mary. I don't know why I couldn't pray that night. Maybe it was my brain's sarcastic way of saying, "Thanks, GOD! I really appreciate this twist. Happy birthday week to me!"

Or, just maybe, this was the first time in my very charmed, blessed life when the scariest things were no longer Lego clowns, but death and serious illness. It was also the first time when I would need to examine my faith and renew my relationship with God.

11

Good Things

Hospital stories can be a real bummer, so for fear of this book becoming a major downer, I will shift gears here and share a list of the many wonderful things that happened to me during my nine-day stay in the hospital:

1. Although my trip to Ireland was canceled, the proprietor of the bed-and-breakfast on the Dingle Peninsula gave us hope and a full refund, writing in an e-mail:

   Good afternoon, Eleanor, and greetings from this most special part of Ireland.

   Many thanks for your message and please pass on my best wishes to your husband for a speedy recovery after his surgery. There will always be a warm bed, a cool pillow, and a wonderful view awaiting you at another time at Pax House.

   Best and warmest wishes.

   John

   This is exactly the kind of e-mail that makes you long for that peaceful trip, whenever it may be.

2. Like at the end of *It's a Wonderful Life*, everyone came to visit and brought me flowers, kindness, and love. It stinks to be sick, but the silver lining is in the amount of love one feels during these times. With all the flowers, calls, and cards coming in, I felt almost like I

was at my own wake, which has always been a secret wish of mine. From the visits of priests to the thoughtful cards from extended family members, it was nice to feel this collective love. My colleagues recorded kind video messages, spearheaded by one of the employees I supervise, and even the dean of the Harvard Graduate School of Education contributed a personal video message, quipping: "Now, if you ever don't want to do anything at work, you can literally say 'I just don't have the stomach for it.'" I work with *great* people!

3. Eventually, after eight days of not eating, I was allowed to eat one slice of toast and a small glass of room-temperature water. While any other day this might seem like a meager pauper's meal, that day it felt like a princely feast. I had never been more excited to eat food in my entire life. It was quite possibly the first (and last) time toast ever tasted better than filet mignon. In fact, as I had missed going to Mass for two Sundays, this was my sustaining bread, and eating it felt transformative. Jesus was definitely present in each flaky, crumbly bite, and I was happy to reacquaint myself with him in this nourishing way.

4. I got to try out the "what if Matt was a reclusive man living in the forest?" look. I've never really enjoyed shaving and occasionally wondered whether I could grow a full, bushy, lumberjack beard. I soon learned that the answer is no, and yet with each passing day, the beard did come in a *little* better. I had hoped that this beard would be a metaphor for my recovery—a harried situation that became slightly less bristly with each passing day. Also, the Boston Red Sox were having a Cinderella year, somehow managing to make the playoffs after coming in last place the year before. Again, more inspiration for my recovery. Oh, and their playoff motto was "Fear the Beard," since they were all growing them.

5. I gained a deep, deep respect for those who work in the health-care industry, from nurses and medical aids to doctors and surgeons. It is not just hard work; it's also not terribly glamorous. I know that many people who spend time in the hospital end up feeling this way, but I gained a special respect for the nurses who catered to both my body and my soul with their kindness and care. I felt like I was given my first "behind the curtain" perspective of the American hospital system, and I was in awe of the people who are its lifeblood.

   One of my favorite possessions during that time in the hospital was a "laugh/sneeze pillow" that one of the nurses made for me out of old linens and surgical tape. With a healing stomach, any sudden movements were quite painful, and laughs and sneezes rely heavily on abdominal muscles. I wasn't laughing much, but sneezes would come on randomly. I would grab my "pillow," hold it against my stomach, and use it as a shock absorber for the pain. Kindness and love were as omnipresent as pain and sadness in this hospital, and it took me a few days to actually realize that.

6. The best day of all was the day I was discharged. I had spent a total of nine straight days in the hospital and was overjoyed with the news that I was being released to the supervision of my wife and honorary nurse. As I was searching for outside-the-hospital clothes, I realized I did not have a clean outfit, so I asked my mother to run down to the gift shop and buy me some clothes. She came back up with a pair of sweatpants and a "Boston Strong" T-shirt, which was the rallying call after the Boston Marathon bombing earlier that spring. I put that shirt on like it was a uniform; I had the best of role models to follow—the victims of the Boston Marathon bombing had seen much, much worse than I had, yet we shared a floor and now a mantra: Boston Strong. That was the goal: to come home, get back to normal, and be strong.

I limped out to the car, took a deep breath of fresh air, and thanked the heavens for the privilege to emerge from a hospital on my own volition. Everything would just go back to normal now—all I wanted was normal.

12

Reintegration

We named him Duck. That was his name because he followed my wife around the house as if she was the mother duck and he was her duckling. He instantly loved her. Before we adopted this seven-pound Australian terrier mix, he had been found marching around the fancy South End of Boston all by himself, looking for food. He was not house-trained, he pulled heavily on the leash, and he barked upon hearing any sound in the house, from a toaster ding to a doorbell ring. He was the kind of dog my mother had warned me of as a child: a high-maintenance stray that you think you want but actually turns out to be more of a challenge than a companion. His saving grace was that he was absolutely the cutest little dog ever, with the kind of face that made it impossible to get mad at him for anything—and trust me, he pushed his luck in those first weeks.

I was sent to the hospital just weeks after adopting Duck. I didn't even really know the guy yet, and he didn't know us that well either. We had sent him off to our friends' house while I was away, but Nell had arranged for him to be there upon our return home.

Everything new seemed old as I climbed the eight steps to our front door. With my wife helping me up the stairs, I felt like we were a time-worn, elderly couple, even though we had been married barely four months. It was almost like we'd been married for years and had seen war and come out on the other side. Our new home was no longer the novelty it had been just a few months prior.

What seemed important and relevant just twelve days earlier I had recategorized as significant but not critical. As I reached to open the door, I wondered, *What will I do with myself? What does this all mean? How will I make peace of this all?*

"Ruff, ruuuuf, ruuuf, ruuuuf, ruuuf!" (I'm not sure how else to describe the barking, snarling, and growling from a little terrier.) We were intruders, hence Duck needed to bark. Upon seeing us both walk into the house, little Duck welcomed Nell with his traditional jumping on top of her, licking her face off, and nipping at her hands. I received a casual glance from him as I slinked my way to the couch.

"Duck, go see Matt . . . Go say hi to Matt!" said Nell, knowing how I could probably use a therapy dog right then.

Sure enough, with lightning speed, little Duck found me on the couch. He proceeded to jump from the floor, stick a perfect landing with the tiniest of paws on my stomach, and then lick the toast detritus from my patchy beard.

Worried his paw may have caught on one of my stitches, I strained to pick up the little guy and place him in a safer place for the both of us.

This return home was the beginning of a very *Odd Couple*-like arrangement for me and Duck, especially as Nell eventually had to return to school, so it would be just me and the seven-pound beast home together. We were basically strangers, but we grew wise to each other's strengths and weaknesses. For example, the dog was actually stronger and much faster than me. He ate a quarter cup of kibble in the morning and another quarter cup at night, which was more food than I would typically consume in the day at that point. His hair was clean, well groomed, and full, while mine was matted and my beard was starting to look like a hairy Greek man's chest. He would take *me* for walks, and at the peak of my facial hair, I looked like a more evolved, though uglier, relative of his species.

When my wife would come home, we'd immediately start competing for her attention. It was the first time in my life that I was actually
jealous of a dog. However, the good thing about a dog—or really about
anything I've tried to care about—is that the longer you spend with
it, the more comfortable and appreciative you become. This was true
with my new condition, my new life, my wife, and my dog. And as I
found myself training Duck not to pounce on my stomach every time
I sat on the couch, I realized he was training me in lessons of patience
each time he did pounce on my stomach. In fact, my whole medical
ordeal had trained me in how to love more deeply and live more fully.
Some of my darkest days birthed many of my brightest realizations on
life: that wisdom is an unexpected side effect of such trauma, one that
is much preferable to the competing side effect, dumping syndrome
(exactly what it sounds like).

So I had been physically transformed and had discovered that a new
internal self was emerging too. Rebuilt, retrained, and developing, I
felt ready to leave my twenties behind in the ashes, and start fresh with
a new decade.

13

Thirty Is the New Seventy

While it would not be taking place on an idyllic peninsula in Ireland, my thirtieth birthday did not go uncommemorated.

A couple days after arriving home, and exactly one year after Elvis visited Houston, Nell artfully arranged for five friends to drop by for an hour. The itinerary included singing "Happy Birthday," posing for a picture, and eating a platter of homemade cupcakes. The memory of that evening lives on like a time capsule in the group photo we took.

In the picture, I'm sitting front and center on the couch with no pants on (they were all too big after I'd lost so much weight), covered up with a blanket. I'm wearing a T-shirt that is the exact shade of blue as a hospital gown, which adds to my sickly aura. I am happy and grinning, but if you look closely you can read the recurring thoughts I was having at the time: *Do they all pity me? Is my butt showing?* To my left, Nell has a bouquet of balloons in one hand and is attempting to hold the squirming Duck in the other. Her face says, "Hold it together! Hold it together!"

Two sets of friends sit to my left and right on the couch, wearing festive *Sesame Street* party hats that Nell bought because she knows I still unabashedly love "the Street." They are clearly good friends who have dropped by to make it a party even though the atmosphere really isn't party-like. To the sides of the couch and on the coffee table are countless bouquets of flowers—like, funeral parlor amounts—wilting away after their previous week's tenure in the hospital.

That photo would end up becoming a teleportation device for me. When I look at it, I can immediately recall how I was feeling the moment I officially turned thirty: safe, surrounded by loved ones, and—probably because of my kinship with the Cookie Monster—hungry!

I wasn't hungry for cookies, though (although scarfing down one cupcake reminded me that I shouldn't be eating such sugary foods); I was hungry for new experiences. I had an insatiable appetite for living thanks to the new perspective on life I had been afforded. Sitting on a couch and in a hospital bed for countless weeks being told what I couldn't do made me want to be a person of action and adventure. This was a new attitude for me—an otherwise cautious, frugal, former twentysomething who was risk-averse even when playing the game of Risk.

After an hour or so of "partying," our guests left, and my wife began our nightly ritual of flushing out the tube that drained an abscess near my stomach, which a visiting nurse had taught her how to do during informal RN training the previous week. Apparently, having the contents of your stomach spill into the rest of your abdomen is pretty serious. While it's trendy to talk about how "good bacteria" and probiotics aid healthy digestion, those little organisms can cause a lot of problems when they somehow escape your digestive system. And for me, all of that bacteria led to some postoperative complications—hence the tube. Essentially, Nell's job was to inject saline into the tube that was attached to the bag on my pants (when I was actually wearing pants). She was also tasked with keeping track of "production." We charted each milliliter of fluid that drained out of me like statisticians on a spreadsheet, tracking any change in trends in a small notebook called "Matt's Health." After this rather intimate procedure, we turned to the more preferable activity of tracking October-playoff baseball stats.

There is something religious about baseball. It's as ritualistic as Mass, with both batboys and altar servers assisting in the grand rite watched by an alternatingly vivacious and bored crowd. They are both stubborn events—multiple walks in one inning with a pitching change is on par with singing all eight verses of the closing hymn after an already-long and meandering homily. However, both are also rewarding events, satisfying that deep-seated drive to lose ourselves in the rhythmic, familiar perfection of the ceremony unfolding before us. They are ripe with depth and steeped into so many of us from our childhoods, building a bridge between yesteryear and today's complexities. Words are closer to poetry when they pertain to baseball, bending more sacred when describing the rhythm of this peculiar game.

Oh, how I loved watching the Red Sox from my hospital bed (and later, my couch)! I found great comfort in the team's success that year, in 2013. I knew all their names, stats, and personal backstories. Who needed reality TV when there were the far more entertaining, unscripted, and beautiful Boston Red Sox? Somehow, they managed to eke out a win, even though the sports columns and betting houses all said they shouldn't have been winning. The Red Sox were scrappy and gritty, fighters to the very last out. They were my bearded brothers, and I was the sick person at home, holding a bouquet of balloons and nibbling on a chocolate cupcake, transfixed to the screen and finding much more meaning and value in a game that had once *just* been a game. Baseball was an escape now; a happy place and a welcome interruption that had enough metaphor, plotline, and subtle complexity to move me through these tough times and help me find faith in what I believed in.

Becoming hungrier with each win—and slightly stir crazy since baseball was my primary distraction while I recovered at home—I felt an internal pull, a craving to be part of this season and to have more positive life disruptions. I didn't know it would take the form of baseball, but I had never been this enthralled with a team or a story, particularly one that seemed to dovetail with exactly what I needed in life at that moment. And what I needed—hope, fun, and faith—was exactly what the Red Sox delivered.

When my beloved Red Sox beat the Detroit Tigers in seven games and punched their entry ticket to the 2013 World Series, my mind was settled: I would surprise my mother and little sister (both of whom are also fans) with tickets to the game. My wife is devoted to the Houston Astros, so it was perfectly fine with her that I would whisk away these two other women to a game that had new layers of meaning for me.

Yes, the tickets cost practically as much as our mortgage. Yes, I hadn't really left the house much in weeks, aside from doctors' appointments and the daily tug-of-war with my feisty terrier. And yes, sitting, standing, and screaming for four hours on a crisp autumn evening was not necessarily medically advisable, but living breeds living, and I had been doing a lot of waiting in the dugout for the previous thirty days. It was nice to deliver good news for once, and both my mother and sister jumped at the opportunity to see game 1 of the World Series at Fenway Park.

And so three weeks after my birthday, arm in arm, the three of us, who had had our fair share of curveballs and wild pitches recently, watched a baseball game that night. It was a sacred affair, and just the right medicine for a heartsick family. We took a lot of pictures, and like that photo from my birthday party, they instantly transport me back to the right-field grandstand seats, especially the picture of me, my mother, and my sister singing along with the loudspeaker to Bob Marley's "Three Little Birds": "Don't worry about a thing / 'Cause every little thing gonna be all right!"

At that moment, everything *was* all right. God's grace washed over us all as baseball and faith played catch in front of our weary eyes.

14

Perspective

"Darling, I hate to ask, but is it possible that you wet the bed?"

This is one of a handful of questions you don't want to hear from your young wife's mouth. In fact, I had been asked this question only once before, and by my mother, but then it was age-appropriate bed-wetting after drinking an unhealthy amount of Hawaiian Punch.

On this occasion, though, I didn't know the answer.

I began patting myself down like a TSA agent and discovered that I was completely wet, lying in a spongy mattress puddle, my shirt and boxer shorts soaked like they had just come out of the washing machine. I'll admit, I even sniffed myself. But that distinguishable salty-sweet fragrance and color of a traditionally wet bed was missing.

Maybe I didn't dry off very well from last night's shower? I wondered.

It was a weird morning, and the event repeated itself the next two mornings. My wife insisted that things were not normal and that we should call the doctor to discuss. I had been out of the hospital for a few weeks then, still recovering at home and very deep into the vast Netflix library.

As luck would have it, I had been experiencing night sweats, a fairly typical sign of postoperative infection. And so I would need doctors to insert a giant needle in me to suck out the lava that had not made its way out of my body. Just like old times, I was back at the hospital for an overnight of heavy-duty IV, antibiotics, and monitoring, as well as a procedure in the morning and discharge the following night, with a new tube, bag, and experience under my belt.

It was no big surprise, then, two weeks later when I sweat the bed again. This time, I knew exactly what to do: call doctor, check in at hospital, identify infection, stay overnight for monitoring, and so on, and so on.

It was my third stint in the hospital in that month, having spent nearly fifteen of the previous thirty days there. After checking in and saying good night to my wife, I folded my hands and waited. I was in a quiet room that I had all to myself (a luxury I came to savor) in what seemed like a remote wing of the hospital, one I had not yet been to. With no baseball to watch that time in the year and it already being somewhat late at night, I decided to feel bad for myself and wallow in the fact that there I was, yet another lonely evening to be followed by an uncomfortable surgery, with who knew how many more to come. I didn't have to be strong for anyone at that point, so I decided to have a bit of a gripe session with God.

It had been only a few weeks earlier that I couldn't even say a Hail Mary; now, I was finding that most of my conversations with him sounded more like tweets to an airline during massive delays:

> @God Come on big man! Not the level of customer service I've come to expect from you. What gives? #fml

> @God Is this some book of Job experiment you're testing out on me? Cool idea, I get the point and I'm actually good now. #ThanksNoThanks

> @God Why. Seriously, why.

Yes, my microprayers to God were less prayerful and more complaint-driven, and my airing of grievances was interrupted only by the occasional passersby on the floor. People watching has never been my favorite activity, but I was open to any distraction as the evening dragged on. I was hungry, tired, and trying to get back to some form of normalcy, yet here I was again, stuck in a cycle: get sick, get better, repeat. I remembered how the surgeon told me that before they stapled me back together, they sprayed water inside me to clean out my body cavity, shaking me around like a mixed drink and then pouring me out.

"With all the nastiness that got inside you, it's likely that small pools of it will still show up and create these infections. It's difficult to know when we've got it all out of you," one of the surgeons told me as I asked about the science behind the procedure.

After contemplating an image of myself as an anesthetized, shaken-not-stirred martini, I decided to go for a walk. I did a small loop around the wing, casually looking in on other rooms, nodding at the nurses, and smiling when I made eye contact with a fellow patient. As I finished the loop back to my room, I stopped suddenly. The sign near the entrance of the wing read: "Transplant."

A tingly feeling percolated up through my body. The crankiness I had been feeling washed away as the faces of the people I had just encountered came to mind. I walked back into my room and got under the covers.

@God Never mind. #blessed

"Everyone on this floor except you is waiting for an organ transplant. Many have been here for quite a while and have a long road ahead of them," my nurse said after I asked her about the floor.

"Some people just don't know how good they have it," she said.

Just when I thought God and I were suffering from major communication issues—so badly that I was considering going on a "break" to reevaluate our relationship—I was given an emotional slap in the face. Tomorrow, I would be going home again. Everyone else on my floor was not as lucky.

Compared to the pain that so many others have faced, my month-long sojourn in Beth Israel Deaconess Hospital in Boston, Massachusetts, was not nothing, but I did not have a terminal illness. I did not have a leg blown off while running a race. I did not have to wait on the transplant floor for the sounds of a helicopter on the roof, hopeful but sad for the person who died when I could live. I was not dying—even more, I did not have to watch a loved one suffering or dying. Many people have suffered much worse experiences than I have, and over longer periods of time and with harsher outcomes, and I bet they did not complain nearly as much as I did about the situation.

I felt like a spoiled brat and petulant fraud, especially compared to the people who suffer far more and likely bitch less to God. In my own small world, my perforated stomach with two post-op infections was front-page news, the headline reading: "The Sky Is Falling—Panic! Post to Facebook!"

Now, I almost wish I could've taken it all back—the complaining, the vocal public suffering, the woe-is-me, the letting everyone know I was OK but still a wounded bird. I truly believe it was by the grace and providence of God that I was placed in that wing on that night so I could have a face-to-face intervention with God to renew our evolving relationship, to reset my attitude and expectations, and to experience a changed outlook, from bitter diva to humble servant. It was odd under the circumstances, but I felt closer to God in that moment.

The next morning, my dedicated, battle-tested wife waited for me outside the ER, brought me home, and held my hand on the couch. A tiny ball of fur jumped up next to us and, for the first time, did not leap on my stomach or accidentally dig his paw into my incision. Rather, Duck plopped himself down in my lap and gave us both the tiniest little licks on our hands, acting more like Lassie than Stephen King's Cujo.

There was hope for us all.

15

Happy Place

The average almond croissant has 27 grams of fat and 366.7 milligrams of sodium. It is the type of treat that *Sesame Street* would call a "sometimes food." Its origins date back to 1839. It pairs very nicely with a slow-drip French roast or even better, a fresh cup of hot chocolate. It is a Sunday morning guilty pleasure for Nell and me, one of those foods you find yourself closing your eyes in enjoyment as you eat.

If you look up a list of the best places in the world to get an almond croissant, it's unlikely that Patisserie Bechler near Monterey, California, will show up. Most people go to Monterey for the beaches, the hiking, the golf, the parks, the art, the possibility of running into Clint Eastwood, but not for the pastries.

Back in 2011, Nell and I attended a wedding in Napa Valley and decided to extend the trip down the coast of California so she could introduce me to her relatives in San Francisco and take me to her grandfather's house in Monterey, which her uncle then owned. It was a place she had loved as a child and had spent many a school vacation visiting. I was excited to meet her family, learn more about her childhood, and explore this part of the country.

While arranging for us to stay at the Monterey house, her aunt sent the following e-mail:

"In case you want a breakfast recommendation, the croissants at Bechler's on 68 on the way to Pacific Grove are *divine*. Have fun!" We made a minor mental note and took off for the coast.

It was one of those special trips with several distinct moments in which you're further convinced that you are going to marry the person you're spending your time with.

"Yes, hello, this is Mr. Weber's assistant. I have just made a reservation for Mr. Weber to dine at your restaurant tonight, but I have a question," said my then-girlfriend Nell.

She had to attend a rehearsal dinner that night and was arranging for me to eat at the nicest steakhouse in the area. I was staring in awe as she continued on the phone.

"Thank you. Yes, Mr. Weber enjoys mashed potatoes with his steak, but I didn't see them on the menu. Would you be able to accommodate that request?"

"Oh, you have to check with the chef first. Sure, yes, I'll hold."

There are fewer ways to a man's heart than through his stomach and by making him feel special. I couldn't stop smiling.

"Oh, the chef will make the special-request mashed potatoes for Mr. Weber's reservation tonight? Wonderful. I'll let Mr. Weber know. I'm sure he'll be most pleased. Thank you!"

It wasn't the exact moment I knew I was going to marry Nell—in fact, I had an inkling on our first date—but that afternoon in Napa was a close second.

Another moment I knew I was going to marry Nell was shortly after the mashed potato phone call and also involved food. Yes, this time it was those delicious, warm, perfectly flaky almond croissants. We were sipping hot chocolate on the back porch of her grandfather's house, looking out at the rising cedars as the soft fog and the pine-scented air drifted through the coast. She was absolutely darling in recollecting her childhood at this home, reminiscing about playing in the Japanese-style gardens, climbing the enormous pine tree with her brother, visiting the nearby navy base with her grandfather, a retired rear admiral, and relishing time with her family. I loved her fondness for family, and felt a strong shared bond in knowing that one day, we too might be a family. The stories, coupled with the croissants and the pines, made this one of my all-time favorite mornings, and one we often refer to as our "peaceful place." When we get stressed or overworked or are having a bad day, it's not uncommon for one of us to joke: "OK, let's go—we're buying tickets right now to Monterey to get a croissant."

Years later, by the time I was home after my third stay in the hospital, we decided we were due for a little getaway. The doctor gave me an all-clear to resume my book tour, and wonder of wonders, there was a conference in Berkeley, just a short drive from Nell's grandfather's house in Monterey.

"Wanna get a croissant in Monterey next month?"

My wife jokingly said yes.

"Good, because I'm serious. I have a conference in Berkeley—you should come with me, and we'll tack on a few extra days to go to your grandfather's house and sit on that porch."

Her eyes lit up.

"We need this, Matt. I can't wait!"

To me the trip was far bigger than a conference and a croissant; it was a triumph of health, happiness, and marital harmony. We had gotten through all this stuff together, and we were going to celebrate having come out on the other side by heading west, seeking all the riches and aspirational promise that come with a California adventure.

Go west, young man! Onward! Croissant ho!

16

Catholic Crowd Surfing

"If the talk is going poorly, I have an emergency backup plan. Trust me."

"Oh, God, you need to tell me what you are going to do, Matt," said my sister Kerry.

We had both been invited to present at a conference in Louisiana and had never given a presentation together before. Kerry is the managing editor of *America*, a Jesuit magazine, and author of the book *Mercy in the City*, which put us both on the speaking circuit. I suppose it was just a matter of time before someone asked us to speak together.

"Seriously, Matt, you need to tell me what you are going to do."

I nonchalantly reached into the front pocket of my suit jacket and pulled out a shiny Hohner harmonica. It was easy to travel with and quite concealable in my pocket.

"Oh, God," she said with a partial eye roll. "OK, fine."

I became an amateur harmonica player (or, more colloquially, harp blower) when I bought my first one at thirteen. The harmonica was cheap, and my dad played it, and so did lesser heroes like Bob Dylan and Bruce Springsteen. It was also the perfect instrument in that it rewards you with minimal training—on the car ride home from buying it, I had already managed to pick up "Jingle Bells." After that, I never looked back. I added to my self-taught repertoire with enthusiasm over the intervening years. As I got older, I would find myself playing on and off again—first at open mics with guitar accompaniment in college, and then, in my most formal association, for two years at the contemporary music Mass while I was a graduate student at Boston College.

When my book tour began in late 2012, I had a unique request from an organization: "Bring your harmonica!" While I had not imagined that my tour would also be the launching point for my fledgling "church rock harmonica" career, I packed it. The talk went well, and at the end of my hour presentation, per request, I pulled out my harmonica and played a short ditty, complete with spontaneous dancing.

It was surprisingly well received, and so I decided to bring my trusty mouth organ to conferences, book talks, and presentations. When appropriate, I'd punctuate the talk with the shortest, most peculiar microconcert.

As a somewhat vulnerable speaker in a strange land, the harmonica in my pocket was like a security blanket—I knew it could help me if I was totally bombing or if I wanted to end the talk on, dare I say, a high note.

As my wife helped me pack for our trip to California, I made sure to include the harmonica, since I was particularly nervous about the talk I would be giving at the University of California Catholic Conference. I would be the morning keynote, hoping to set a strong tone for the two-day conference that included more than four hundred college students from the UC system and other nearby schools—all of whom were traveling to Berkeley to discuss the conference theme, "Let There Be Light!"

I'm typically a nervous flier, but our journey to California cradled both of us comfortably away from the turbulence and cold of the east, and into the warm embrace of the west. The plan was to quickly visit with Nell's cool uncle and aunt in San Francisco, borrow his car to drive to Berkeley for the night, deliver the talk the next morning, and then head to Monterey for three days of unprogrammed bliss.

The students and conference organizers couldn't have treated me better. In fact, the life of the Catholic author on a book tour offers a small taste of what it's like to be a rock star: airport pickups, comped Internet in the hotel rooms, and local news coverage. I am even referred to as "Mr. Weber" on occasion, which always makes me wonder if my dad is standing behind me.

After being treated to pizza and graciously shown around the school grounds, Nell and I were delivered to my hotel room in a historical building on campus. While I was usually alone on these talks, it was fun having my wife around not just to enjoy time with, but also for her to hear and see, for example, what "I've got to go give a book talk in Pittsburgh this weekend" actually means.

I woke up the next morning feeling filled with the Holy Spirit, excited to give this talk. It was as if the theme "Let There Be Light!" was providential for my soul at that point in life. My wife and I walked over from our hotel room, up a big hill and a big set of stairs leading to the hall where I would be giving my talk.

"Do you mind if we get brunch with my friend from high school who's at law school here after the talk, then head to Monterey?" asked Nell.

"Of course! I can't usually eat much before a talk anyways," I said. I was in one of those uncharacteristic, early morning giddy moods. Nell could've asked for a pony and a pink Corvette and I would've said a resounding "Yes!" without thinking twice.

Something was in the air that fine Californian morn. The conference was pregnant with an unmistakable energy that only a group of faith-filled, on-fire-with-the-Holy-Spirit college students could generate. I felt honored to be part of the conference, and as I was standing backstage being introduced, I felt like Bruce Springsteen about to take center stage at the Meadowlands. I patted my harmonica to make sure it was still there, did a quick sign of the cross, and made my way through the curtain for the beginning of my sixty-minute talk.

I was back! For about fifty-nine minutes, I was my best self. The message, the audience, the jokes, the flow—all the things you would want to be firing on all cylinders *were* during this talk. Such a perfect synchronization is rare in the speaking circuit world, let along during a comeback performance after several months on the disabled list.

Now I could've ended a few minutes early, walked down the stairs of the stage, signed my books, and then drove off into the sunset with my wife. But God had different plans for me that morning.

Perhaps it was that perfect cocktail of adrenaline, hubris, happiness, and a double shot of the Holy Spirit, but in the last minute of my allotted time, I decided to reach into my pocket.

"Perhaps we can end our hour together with a thematically appropriate song. Any requests?" I had alluded to playing the harmonica earlier in the talk, so it should have been no surprise that I would pull just that out of my pocket.

"This Little Light of Mine!" someone shouted from the front row.

That was exactly what I had hoped for. I had even practiced it the night before, thinking there was a strong chance I might play it during a conference themed "Let There Be Light."

I held the microphone to the harmonica, and after a quick lick of the lips, the grand finale began. Singing, dancing, jubilation ensued! The crowd got to their feet—and for a fleeting moment I was St. Bruce of Springsteen jamming with God on the stage as the light inside me shone brighter than it had been in many, many months. I couldn't contain my energy as Catholic rock 'n' roll flowed through my soul and the Holy Spirit kept time with a strong bass note.

And then, with very little input from my brain, in the middle of the final verse, I jumped off the stage. My intention was to stick the landing and finish the song among the crowd, sign my books, and drive off into the sunset, as mentioned.

I was only half successful.

I heard a distinct crack as I landed on the floor and tumbled in a partial somersault down the middle aisle. It was very clear to me that I had just broken my foot in front of four hundred people; I had become just another statistic among the very few harmonica-related injuries in the world. But I was pretty sure I was the only one who knew it was broken, so I had to make a quick decision:

Stop playing. Seek medical help. Leave on stretcher.

Or:

Keep playing. Get up off the ground. Finish the song. Pretend like nothing had happened.

I am sure it was the adrenaline coursing through my veins that helped numb the pain, but somehow I managed to pull myself up, keep playing the song, strut back to the stage with far less Springsteen swagger, finish the song, take a few questions, and hobble to the book-signing area, where good-byes and thank-yous were had.

My wife knew something was up.

"Are you OK, sweetie? That looked like a nasty fall."

"First of all, it was a purposeful, yet unsuccessful, stage jump, not a fall. And second of all, my foot is broken. Can you drive me to a hospital now?"

As I was limping down the stairs of the auditorium and out the building, I explained to her that I would've hated for the previous fifty-nine minutes to be ruined in the final minute when the speaker had to be rushed to the hospital because he foolishly jumped off the stage while playing the harmonica, perhaps affording a new joke of changing the theme to "Let There Be Flight." While I had made a totally boneheaded move, I didn't want it to be the defining moment of the morning—the "wardrobe malfunction" of an otherwise good Super Bowl halftime show.

It was a long walk back to the hotel, down those many hills and stairs, and one on which my wife acted as both physical and emotional support.

"Are you sure it's broken, not just sprained? How can you tell for sure?" Having been my nurse, confidante, and best friend through the illness of the previous few months, and during our years together, Nell knew that I could be tough but sometimes prone to overstatement, especially when my emotions were high.

"It's broken," I said to her through clenched teeth.

"OK, sweetie," said Nell. "Sweetie" felt less sweet as she said it. I had the broken foot, but I could see her spirit beginning to crack with another potential tour of nursing duty on the horizon.

"Let me text my friend and let her know we'll be missing brunch."

This was an old friend my wife rarely sees, and she was really looking forward to visiting her. We were both hungry, and my foot wasn't going to get any more broken. I figured I had at least a half hour left of adrenaline streaming through my body before the acceptable level of pain would yield to excruciating agony.

"Nell, I insist that we still go to brunch. We will try to enjoy this last hour of normalcy."

She had been through a lot. She was about to go through a good deal more with something far less serious but equally inconvenient. We didn't know how to react to this one. We just felt dumbfounded that our triumphant trip celebrating healing and redemption had actually bred another form of broken. Initially, it just seemed comical.

What would've naturally been very tasty French toast was in fact the object of my scorn as my adrenaline decreased. I didn't say a whole lot as my wife quickly caught up with her friend and offered a very reasonable excuse for why we had to leave early.

"This guy has had a rough year. We're going to go to the emergency room and hopefully be surprised to learn that it's not a broken foot!"

She was the eternal optimist, and I loved her for it. We took to the car and—like old veterans of the mercurial game of life—drove to the nearest urgent-care center. This time we knew the problem and had a sense of the solution.

"Yup, it's definitely broken," the doctor said after an X-ray. "You'll be in a boot and on crutches for at least eight weeks."

And that wasn't even the worst news I'd get that week: the almond croissant place was closed.

17

A Crutch with Crutches

There are a few activities I would not recommend doing while operating crutches:

1. Traversing on sand along the beach. It is an exercise in frustration, incredibly inefficient, and poorly suited for a romantic Pacific Ocean sunset moment with your wife.

2. Going through airport security. Also, finding a suitable place for them in the overhead luggage compartment or under the seat involves a good deal of spatial negotiation.

3. Shoveling snow with "help" from your leashed dog, who is in dire need of outdoor time. Crutches have limited traction on ice and do not allow for great stability when being pulled in another direction.

4. Quietly sneaking into Mass, fifteen minutes late. There will be squeaking . . .

However, aside from the obvious, crutches can really enhance one's life, too:

1. They make it easier to flush toilets and push elevator buttons.

2. People hold open doors and vacate seats on the subway when you hobble by.

3. They provide necessary upper-body workouts and well-timed abdominal toning, especially after a traumatic loss of muscle and mass.

4. They are good training for when we all become part-human, part-machine cyborgs.

The line between comedy and tragedy is thin. The cold winter that followed my perforated stomach and then broken foot yielded laughter and cursing, ecstasy and agony. I was both comforted and saddened by one of my favorite lines from the writer Khalil Gibran's work *The Prophet*:

> Some of you say, "Joy is greater than sorrow," and others
>   say, "Nay, sorrow is the greater."
> But I say unto you, they are inseparable.
> Together they come, and when one sits alone with you at
>   your board, remember that the other is asleep
>   upon your bed.

This was my winter of discontent. My brain rationally said that again, compared to my floormates in the transplant wing, I was still in good shape and should not be complaining. Yet, as a flawed and cranky human being, I found myself wallowing at not being able to shower standing up or help out with chores around the house. Yes, I actually wanted to do chores!

Poor Nell began the second semester of a very challenging doctoral program with her husband yet again in constant need of her assistance. In almost six months of marriage we really hadn't been a normal couple yet. My dreams of marriage being *Leave It to Beaver* were turning into the challenges of *Modern Family*. I was by all accounts difficult to be around, trying to live as normally as possible but never really succeeding (e.g., trying to shovel, walk the dog, help around the house on a broken foot). In trying to help, I was actually causing more frustration for myself and my wife.

"Why are you shoveling the snow in crutches wearing gym shorts? Are you *crazy?*" Nell exclaimed in exasperation, coming home from a long day of classes to see me out in the driveway pushing a shovel with one hand.

"I'm just trying to help us! God!" I screamed back, throwing the shovel to the ground. We had been polite and guarded in our frustration up until this point. She picked up the shovel and starting shoveling furiously. In slow motion, I tried to grab the shovel away from her so I could finish. But I was out-maneuvered and left standing trying to convince her she had too much work to do and I was not a total invalid. To prove my point, I began pushing snow off the sidewalk using two very inefficient shovels—my crutches—that cleared tiny, two-inch rows at a yeoman's pace. The dog started barking, knowing Nell had returned home. I was yelling and Nell was yelling back. We had all hit our boiling point on one of the coldest nights of the year.

"Stop being stubborn and let me just do this," she said as she finished the sidewalk.

There were a few nights like that that winter. But we found that in those tense moments, sometimes steam had to be released for our relationship to continue to grow and thrive.

That same month, I had also returned to work, but I found myself in a position of having to explain why I was now on crutches. It was awkward. Coming from me, that kid who was never sick or missed a day of school from kindergarten to twelfth grade, my identity was partially built around my sense of toughness, grit, and resilience. I had never had to account for any absence or illness before, and now in my thirtieth year, I was constantly having to explain to people that, yes, I was injured, sick, and broken once more.

The first time I went back to work, the story involved showing off a scar and a fantastical account of ulcers, emergency surgery, and stomach removal. It wasn't pleasant, but I sort of felt like a badass. The second time coming back to work after my four-day "vacation" to Monterey was far more embarrassing. I had to determine just how much detail to give when describing my intentional stage dive, while playing harmonica. To most, I would just say, "I fell off a stage"—not a lie, since jumping could technically be considered a controlled fall. Luckily, I have very supportive coworkers who helped and encouraged me along the way, and were flexible with my limited mobility on crutches while in the office.

At home, sorrow and joy continued that grand waltz. Most nights involved warm, homemade soups and cuddling on the couch; others, frustrating juggling acts of managing rides, appointments, dog walks, dinners, and life. "In good times and in bad" started to blend together on a daily basis. And so, to give my wife even the shortest of a respite from my malaise, I decided to seek the support of another woman's love and attention: my mother.

18

Faith Is Like a Frozen Owl

As the days grew darker, the snow seemed to fall heavier and wetter. It was no longer just a bad winter; it had been rebranded as the polar vortex, a serious-sounding name to rival the sexy El Niño or La Niña.

I was growing weary, more agitated, and more aware of my crotchetiness toward my wife. I was an oversized, crutch-wielding Tiny Tim, but with Scrooge's demeanor. I was not looking forward to the holidays, was less generous with others, and was a jerk on the road when it came to honking, passing, and showing any patience. The days passed. Netflix movies all had the same plot, and it pained me to see my wife return from a long day of classes only to find me sprawled on the couch, about to begrudgingly ask for food, clean clothing, and undeserved kindness.

During a phone call with my parents one night, I decided I should diffuse my crabbiness among my loved ones rather than focusing it on my poor newlywed spouse. After all, my mother always told me, "I'll love you even if you become a bank robber and go to jail." I was neither, but still very unlovable at the moment to anyone but those required biologically or legally to put up with me. So that weekend, we headed to my parents' home in western Massachusetts.

Even if you live relatively close and visit often, it's still always a little strange to head back to your childhood home. Something usually has changed. One year my dad had all the trees removed around our house. To him, the trees posed a risk of falling on the roof during an ice storm, but to me, those trees were goal posts for soccer games, pull-up bar branches, and family hammock holders in the summertime. It wasn't just that the trees were gone, so was the possibility of re-creating memories from a happy childhood.

But this time, it was not the home that had changed. It was me. I was different in how I saw the world—everything old was new, and everything new, I wished was old news. Memories from childhood flooded back, and mine were all filled with sunny days and good health. I hated being sick, pitied, helpless, and a hindrance for so long. I was rarely amused or interested in anything new.

As we turned down my parents' street and looked out the car window, I was surprised to catch a glimpse of the most beautiful bird on the edge of my family's lawn. I couldn't tell exactly what type of bird it was, but it appeared large, had pure-white feathers, and looked resplendent. I noticed it wasn't moving and decided to investigate as my first order of business.

I inched up to confirm it would not in fact wake up and maul my face off. After the year I had been having, I considered that a greater possibility than usual. The bird turned out to be the most beautiful owl I had ever seen, and it was very dead. Now, I have seen plenty of dead animals on the road: squirrels, robins, skunks, deer—you name it. As I pass by them, I wonder how they died. I usually assume they were on the receiving end of a car with ill timing, and then I move on with my day. But I became enamored of this owl—I'm not sure if it was because I had never seen a dead owl before, or because this owl was just so strikingly majestic. Perhaps I even felt some ownership of it, or obligation to tend to it, since its fateful last breaths had occurred on my family's soil. Maybe it had once even known my old goalposts or pull-up bar. I was reminded of the Latin maxim *sic transit gloria mundi*, "the glory of the world is fleeting." This once majestic bird was dead; its glory had "fleeted." I slinked to the house and found a couch to perch atop.

The following day, I was curious about how my owl friend had fared overnight. Usually a dead carcass attracts those tiny friends that allow the circle of life to take place (yes, much of my biology knowledge is from *The Lion King*). To my surprise, the owl was the same: in the same position, the same color, and still so stunning. While I am neither a meteorologist nor a biologist, I deduced that the polar vortex temperatures were actually keeping this bird perfectly preserved, and that maybe, just maybe, the glory of the world (or this bird) was not so fleeting. Perhaps this beauty could be preserved forever and this once majestic animal could see its beauty live on, captured in a moment but still alive in splendor.

The new goal of my weekend became rescuing this owl. Not like Lazarus, or the movie *Pet Sematary*, but I would rescue it from decay. My immediate plan was to scoop it up with a shovel, put on gloves, encase it in Saran Wrap, put it in the freezer, contact a taxidermist, have it cleaned, stuffed, and mounted, and then proudly display this owl in my home, hoping my wife didn't mind a stuffed owl in the house and think I had completely lost my mind. In my head it was already a symbol, another instance of meaning making; the stuffed owl would be a reminder for me that a negative thing can breed a positive, and that we can feel inspiration and impact long after death. I was that owl, and I wanted to help myself. Yes it seemed contrived, but I was searching for small moments of inspiration, and this dead bird inexplicably resonated with me.

Heartened and excited about a new pet project (pun intended), I moved as fast as I could to my parents' computer to Google "local owl taxidermy."

Within seconds of research I yelled at the screen, "Damn you, Internet! Damn you for ruining my plan!"

Several web pages confirmed that there is an up to $25,000 fine for anyone who attempts to even move, let alone stuff, an owl—unless of course you are a state employee or member of a Native American nation. And so, my plan was foiled practically at its inception, and the owl became merely a fallen friend to visit for the next few days. I found myself checking in with the owl in the way I used to check in with God—perhaps I was seeing a bit of my faith wrapped up in this bird. Was I trying to preserve a once-glorious faith life and nail it to the wall to remind myself of how things used to be? Or was my faith inevitably a decaying carcass that had lost its beauty and breath amid so much pain?

I eventually came to understand that maybe, like the owl, I was transforming myself. The world might pick at me and pluck my feathers and freeze my flesh, but it would always be up to me to see something there that is not death. It would be up to me to see beyond death, beyond heartbreak and past pain, toward healing. To take a dead owl, realize it cannot be made beautiful forever (both legally and biologically), and know that it is also a fact of life—and oddly a fact of faith. Man's greatest search for meaning lies in that link between life and faith, the biological and the spiritual. Was this a lesson in growing wiser in my faith from God? *Whoo* knows.

19

Love, Actually, Overwhelmingly

Good afternoon, Eleanor, and greetings from Dingle.

Many thanks for your message and I am delighted that your husband is doing well. How fast the time goes by. We do have availability for Monday 17th and Tuesday 18th March, and I can offer you a choice of bedrooms for these two requested nights.

Best and warmest wishes to yourself and of course your husband.

John.

Nell had yet another surprise up her sleeve: a rescheduled trip to Ireland, booked before I broke my foot but with perhaps just enough time for me to get off my crutches before I'd get on the plane.

"It's going to be close," my orthopedist said, after I asked whether I'd be on crutches for our trip, or if we should, yet again, delay our voyage.

"If you just take it easy, I think you'll be fine to walk by then," he concluded. I found it ironic that while my ancestors desperately tried to flee Ireland, two generations later, I was having serious trouble just getting there. To me, it would be more than a vacation; it would be a homecoming—a place to be reminded of where my family actually came from, to connect with my roots, and to walk in the path of my great-grandparents. I also wanted to say thank you to a generation who worked really hard to get to a new land that I have enjoyed.

With a German name like Weber, you might be surprised that I am mostly Irish, raised in a very Irish American section of Springfield, Massachusetts. All my friends' parents were police or firefighters, and my mother called me her Irish prince. Because of my last name, though, I felt like I wasn't totally part of the club, so I always tried to play up my connection to the motherland.

Nell is of Irish heritage too, and she is really attached to her Irish name, O'Donnell. It really can't get more Irish than that, but when we were married, she still wanted to change her name to Weber and make O'Donnell her middle name. She did this out of love and out of a desire for unity, saying while she loved O'Donnell, she loved me more, and wanted us to be connected in name too. I suggested that maybe we should both change our last names to O'Weber and be the only O'Webers in the phone book. (For my younger readers, before the Internet there was a big book with phone numbers in it that everyone got. It was called a phone book.) Or maybe I could be Matt O'Donnell? She said she loved me for suggesting that (she calls me her "little feminist") but was still looking forward to being a Weber. So, she began the long journey of officially becoming a Weber according to the Social Security Administration . . . and the Department of Motor Vehicles, the U.S. Department of State (passports), credit-card companies, e-mail accounts, banks, frequent-flier accounts, loyalty clubs, and on and on. In the months after the wedding, I saw Nell become a Weber—very slowly, yet officially—and I was astonished by the amount of work, time, and effort it took to make that change.

"*Weber* has been good to me, but I really wish this was at least an alphabetical upgrade for you. Also, people will always spell it with two *b*s, mispronounce it, and make many references to the grill company," I said.

"I'm going to miss having an apostrophe," she said. "But I want to do this and I love us."

That was my wife's attitude in a nutshell: "I love us." She was self-less, caring, sympathetic, and supremely kind. She changed her name not because it was tradition or the right thing to do, but because she loved me and wanted to be closer to me. That love is baked into every single moment of our courtship, our marriage, and this book. She embodies a sense that in marriage, we are no longer just individuals, but this beautiful new partnership that makes decisions and lives life as an "us." Our love was the most precious gift we had, and it was something we held sacred and holy, present in acts big and small. I had been on the receiving end of it for quite some time and was looking to reciprocate.

"Matthew O. Weber. Is that how you would like your license to read?" said the man at the DMV.

"Yes!" I chirped gleefully, holding my license with my new middle name: O'Donnell. I had made it official. After thirty years, this Irish prince was part of the club—not just the Irish-sounding-name club, but the best club I could've ever imagined: partnership with Nell O'Donnell Weber.

This was all to be a surprise for Nell since she didn't know I was undertaking this stealth mission on my lunch breaks and Friday after-noons. Once I had the license I wanted to surprise her over dinner. On the day I got my license, I had planned a dinner at one of our favorite Italian restaurants. We sat down, chatted casually over bread, and then I told her that there was something I needed to tell her.

She looked at me, concerned.

"I'm not the man you think I am," I said seriously, trying to hold a straight face.

Blood drained from her face.

"There is something important about me that you do not know."

She sat back and said, "I'm pretty sure you're joking, but please hurry up and tell me whatever you need to tell me."

I pulled out a document from my pocket and, feigning reluctance, handed it to her across the table.

She snapped it up, likely wondering whether I was in witness protection or a convicted felon.

It took her a minute to figure out what she was looking at and why it was so meaningful.

"Matthew O. Weber! *O* . . . as in O'Donnell?"

I let out a long-overdue smile and relished the great joy and happiness on her face as she pored over the license. I handed her the social security card from my other pocket as double confirmation.

"I'm an O'Donnell now and could not be happier to be one!" I said with a slight mist coming over my eyes as I leaned in to give my wonderful wife a kiss.

She was a Weber, and I was an O'Donnell. She was an O'Donnell, and I was a Weber. It just seemed right. We had each other during a time in our lives when partnership was critical, when love took many forms, and when God was about to guide two pale-skinned Irish kids to experience our shared ancestral homeland for the very first time.

20

Many Faces

The world is charged with the grandeur of God.
—Gerard Manley Hopkins

For most of my life, I had a very traditional understanding of God's image—that is, how I see God and picture God in my limited understanding of the creator. A few obvious and not so obvious images come to mind:

1. God as an old man with long locks and a white robe, seated on a throne in a cloud. This is likely the image most people initially conjure of God, surrounded by angels and a harp-playing entourage in the clouds. God is probably extending a hand outward and has a serious face, as if troubled by some business going on below.

2. God as a voice from above, a booming voice, like James Earl Jones, calling out to us in serious or sensitive ways.

3. An angry God, like the depiction in the mosaic at the Basilica of the National Shrine of the Immaculate Conception in Washington, DC. Looking up at this giant depiction for the first time, I was actually afraid of Jesus, which scared me, because I was not usually afraid of Jesus. I know he was pretty upset when he threw the money changers out of the temple, but the Jesus I think of is typically nice Jesus.

4. Nice Jesus—essentially the Jesus in every Catholic coloring book. He talks to children or prays, or does things that any nice,

thirtysomething fellow would do. He is kind and forgiving, smart and serious, and smiling.

5. The Holy Spirit as a dove, or more like a ghost bird with a special glow, like a dove bitten by a radioactive spider. Most other iconography of the Holy Spirit is usually just a beam of light (i.e., think Tinkerbell at the beginning of the *Wonderful World of Disney*).

6. Apocalypse God, who throws fireballs and lightning bolts, who is big, like Zeus, and who is angry that the world hasn't been good. Apocalypse God sits on a cloud and is not to be reasoned with, since we've already had our chance.

7. Grand Canyon and/or Rainbow God, who doesn't take any human form. Rather, God rests silently and peacefully in the beauty and perfection of nature's most awe-inspiring things—those sunsets, waterfalls, vistas, or adorable puppies that give you chills and make you feel connected to something bigger.

Throughout my life, it had been very easy for me to connect with these classic renditions of God. At church I would pray toward the crucifix or a statue of an image I had known and loved since childhood. If I wanted to feel closer to God, I knew how to find God in the familiar, in the conventional staples of my mind. Yet a mercurial year of ups and downs led me not just to question his role in my life but also to try to find new ways to engage with God.

Quite frankly, I wasn't praying comfortably or clearly and was getting very little out of Mass. I couldn't figure out why God decided I had to have such a rough year. I was looking for God in all the old places—Mass, the rosary, simple evening prayer—but was unsuccessful in renewing my connection with God. I would have moments of inspiration, but they were short lived. Even so, I loved that God was always by my side; he knew me, he knew everything, and he could relate, like a companion on a road trip through life. During the first twenty-nine years of my life, God was my chatty companion and navigator, but in my thirtieth year, I felt like God was still present in the car but had fallen asleep, leaving me with some comfort of companionship, but also the stress of not having a copilot and confusion as to why he would put me in this situation.

Enter Nell O'Donnell Weber. She was the person who had been by my side, knew me, knew everything I had gone through, and could relate to my pain. She took care of me, helped me, loved me, and endured me when I was difficult. She was my rock and my rock star, my confidante, and my best friend. At a time when I felt most distant from God, I felt closest to Nell. And yet somehow I didn't connect that everything Nell was doing for me was Christ-like, that God was even more present through the love of my wife, the life of my love. I couldn't see God because God was Nell, God was my wife. I had discovered a deeper understanding of the creator through Nell. Now this book may be starting to sound like a weird religious soap opera, but essentially, I finally saw my wife as the living, breathing manifestation of God's work in the everyday minutiae of my life. God is in all things, takes different forms, and is not always clearly revealed to us. Sure, God is ubiquitous, and so God is everywhere, but air is everywhere and we don't always feel the wind or breeze. We will often separate, file, and categorize our understandings in life—we look for sense and meaning by placing it into the familiar. If something doesn't fit the bill or isn't obvious, we might miss it.

Now, adding an eighth item to my list of images of God, and in bold, permanent ink: Nell O'Donnell Weber, my divine wife.

21

My Internet Friends Named Francis

Every day at 3 a.m., I get an e-mail from someone I don't know. It is not spam, or from a company asking me to buy little blue pills. The subject line is typically just "E-Mail," and the message is short, two or three sentences long.

They come from a man named Francis, and according to his first e-mail, I met him on my book tour at a conference in Massachusetts. I don't know what he looks like, I don't remember meeting him, but he is the person I can count on for an e-mail every single day.

A typical week's conversation:

Hi Matt,

How did your conference go? Good luck. Went to see my cousin Bob at the nursing home yesterday. He has Parkinson's. He is the same. There was thunder, lightning, and rain yesterday. Going for coffee with friends this morning. Going to lunch at Panera. Have a good day.

Francis

Hi Francis,

Conference was good but long. I love Panera—my favorite soup is the broccoli and cheddar. Bad weather delayed my plane yesterday—glad to be back in Boston.
Hope you are well,

Matt

Hi Matt,

Glad your conference went good. I love Panera too. Enjoyed my visit with my friends yesterday. I also like the broccoli and cheddar soup. It rained yesterday. It is raining here now. Have a good weekend.

Francis

Hi Francis,

You too!! Happy Memorial Day too!!!

Hi Matt,

Happy Memorial Day. It finally stopped raining. It is sunny here. Went with my cousin after church to Walmart. At least I got out. Nothing planned today. Wish I had somewhere to go for a picnic. Have a good day.

Francis

Hi Francis,

No picnic for me either . . . just a day to rest and relax. Harvard has its graduation this week—will be busy times. It's been cold and feels like winter—doesn't Mother Nature know it's almost summer!?

Hope you are well and enjoying the good sun.
Matt

Hi Matt,

Yesterday, I took a walk just to get out to enjoy the nice weather. I relaxed too. My cousin Ted and I are going for coffee. It is supposed to warm up this week. I am well. Have a good day.

Francis

Hi Francis,

Great! It's supposed to be 90 degrees in a few days—HOT!! Hope you have air conditioning . . .

Hi Matt,

Have good news. I'm going to be a great-uncle in October. My nephew and his wife, Jerri, are expecting. Have counseling, and going for coffee with Dustin, a friend. I have central air conditioning. Have a good day.

Francis

Francis was consistent and reliable—a rare Internet friend older than seventy (I think?). I count on hearing from him every morning when I wake up. I must say, I didn't expect him to send me an e-mail every day. I quickly deduced that he wasn't dangerous or creepy, just a nice old man who liked telling me about his day via e-mail. I decided that I would reciprocate.

In fact, Francis started writing to me just a few months after Pope Francis was chosen as the new pope. At that time, I would eat up everything Pope Francis was saying, and I engaged with his homilies, appearances, and Twitter account. Some might say that I was mildly obsessed with the pope—I even bought my mother a giant framed portrait of him that she has since put above the mantle as the centerpiece of our family home's hearth. I tried in every way to be like Pope Francis, and I loved his simple yet powerful message of helping out those in need and loving all who we come into contact with.

And so, two months later when I started getting e-mails from an old man named Francis, I thought perhaps this was an opportunity to be like Pope Francis with another Francis, to be kind and create community for all people, friend or stranger.

In fact, one of the first things that came to mind after I knew I was going to be in the hospital for a while was to make sure I e-mailed Francis, letting him know I wouldn't be writing.

In hospital now. Stomach surgery.

Have been here for four days. Say a prayer if you can.

Matt,

Hope you are feeling better. I pray for you. Took walks yesterday.
Hope things go good.

Francis

It was the kind of unique friendship that just seemed to work—like the little bird that sits on the back of his rhinoceros best friend at the zoo. Every day, even today as I'm writing this book, I'm reminded of the message of Pope Francis in a daily e-mail from this other Francis. My friend Francis is a reminder of the goodness and kindness in the world, and of an old man's search for community and connection. In many ways, Pope Francis does this every day in his embrace of the world's Catholics and all people, most of whom he doesn't know personally. And this is what God does every day—calling us to provide subtle reminders of love, support, and kindness in whatever way we can. How could I not respond in kind for just one person?

I know it is very en vogue to be writing about Pope Francis these days. You may in fact be wondering if, with this being printed by a Jesuit publisher, I am contractually obligated to include a chapter about Pope Francis in my book. Obviously not, but there's certainly a sense of all things Francis converging upon me in a year when I needed some saintly assistance (Assisi-tance?).

Pope Francis made it cool to be Catholic again, and he has recalibrated what people think Catholicism means. In the past, whenever I met people and they found out I was Catholic, topics like the abuse scandal and *The Da Vinci Code* always came up first. Now, Pope Francis is the first topic, and he's brought up with respect and admiration from people of all faiths. His reverence transcends religions, and many hold him in the same universal esteem as they do the Dalai Lama.

My Internet friend Francis showed me the power of the Catholic community. Francis is the reminder and challenge to answer any call that God may send out, and to respond with a growing admiration for that which is simple and ordinary. There are millions of things that Catholics do every day that are not sexy or celebrated, written about or tweeted. From praying for a stranger to late-night chats about broccoli and cheddar soup, God is in those details, too.

A third Francis—the animal-loving St. Francis—was even present in my life in how I loved little Duck, who taught me patience and discipline through training and taking mandatory walks at the beginning, middle, and end of the day. These were times when I would gather my thoughts, pray, pick up poop, and examine how I could be a better person.

During my most difficult year, the perfect storm of Franci (plural of Francis?)—pope, friend, and saint—was my lifeboat of hope and faith in a choppy sea. I was grateful to Francis for his consistency and kindness, Pope Francis for his message and call to live your best self, and St. Francis, present in little Duck, calling me to look inward. I still find myself examining the ubiquity of Francises in my life—although at that time, Nell and I would be getting a heavy helping of another saint, St. Patrick, very soon.

22

Dublin, Finally!

"They're probably in the other one," I said as I stepped over a grave-stone, motioning to the cemetery around the bend in the road.

There are two churches in Waterford, County Kerry, in Ireland. Nell and I were looking for stones that read Brennan, so we could say a prayer for my mother's grandparents in the town they had emigrated from more than a hundred years earlier.

"We will find them if we have to look all day," Nell said, equally determined to meet the people who were now part of her family tree too.

It was an idyllic day, full of sunshine and clear skies. The greens were even greener and the sheep more sheepish than I expected across a countryside that is exactly as advertised by every postcard and Lucky Charms commercial I'd ever seen. We had made it down to Waterville on the correct side of the road with intermittent stops at castles, beau-tiful vistas, and even a small roadside town that had won the "Most Beautiful Town in Ireland" award.

A few days earlier, we had arrived in Dublin on the eve of St. Patrick's Day, of all days. Our day was bookended by what I assume is a very typical Irish way: church and Guinness. Mass was lovely, as was my first sip of alcohol since my stomach surgery. I'm not a huge fan of Guinness, I prefer the record book to the drink, but I had just bought an Aran sweater, was sitting in a pub with live music, and everyone else was drinking Guinness, so I figured, *Why not? I'm home.* (I ordered a Coke later, solidifying my Irish *American* heritage.)

As the music played and I stomached a very bitter but popular stout, I looked over at my wife. She was sitting in the chair next to me, mapping out our route and pouring over the tour book, brochures, and maps we had just acquired. She fit right in otherwise—a perfect archetype of the fair-skinned, freckled Irish lass, beautiful in every way, again and again. With her by my side, I felt like I fit in better by association, and that extended beyond Ireland; I felt cozy and comfy in life as her husband, better together than alone. Life was near perfect at this moment; I had an almost-healed foot and a stomach that was not eroding at its first contact with hops and barley.

This was the good times; this was health. Rare is it that I ever soaked in what many fortunate people consider a proverb, that whole "you don't know what you've got till it's gone." I had always expected everything to be grand, perfect, the best. I was an unapologetic idealist and optimist, and I had suffered very little loss in close to three decades. As I closed my eyes in that moment, I savored the simple pleasures of walking and eating, drinking and sitting up. I realized Nell also fell into this category of essentials I should never take for granted.

"Let's go to the other church. It looked closed but I'm sure they still have a cemetery," Nell said.

Back in Waterville, we got into our rental car, drove a few feet across the street, and came upon what looked like an abandoned church—abandoned not in the twelfth century, but more like in 2005. We were surprised to find that the door was open and unlocked, and inside were the remnants of what was once a modest town church. I scoured the walls for the Brennan family name in the stained glass and in the list of parishioners. I even fantasized that I'd stumble upon some old photo with a man who looked exactly like me, yet it would read "Mr. Brennan 1905"—in my fantasy, though, I'd have a cool, sentimental moment, not a paranormal, "I've been dead all along" moment like at the end of *The Shining*.

Alas, to no avail did we find Brennans. We went outside, looking for gravestones with the name Brennan in the second old cemetery of the day. Like kids diving into a word search, we went row by row, searching for where my ancestors might've been laid to rest. As our search was wrapping up, Nell let out an enthusiastic squeal—the most excitement this cemetery had likely seen in a while.

"Matt, look!"

It was like when Indiana Jones found the Ark of the Covenant or the Holy Grail, a spiritual moment capping the end of a long quest. There was the name *Brennan*, written in bold, old-fashioned typeface.

It was the only one we found so we assumed it had to be "our" Brennan. Here it was, the family plot. I looked out from their final resting place, resting atop a big hill, and saw a beautiful sun setting over the ocean that had brought the Brennans to America, where they eventually met Sheas and Martins, who eventually met Webers, one of whom eventually met an O'Donnell and became an O'Donnell himself, and who traveled with that O'Donnell back across the sea to see a Brennan. In my mind, the family tree was in full bloom, and God was visible in this grand growth of roots and branches.

"Let's say a prayer," I said.

Solemnly, after a prayer, we left that place and traveled on to Dingle, where we finally met the man who had thrice promised us "warm beds and cold pillows" in his picturesque bed-and-breakfast, Pax House. He would have little knowledge of just how meaningful his e-mails were to me: they represented the promise of peace during a tumultuous year.

Moved and inspired by how connected we felt to Ireland, Nell and I even picked up hitchhikers en route to Dingle, throwing caution to the wind, as being helpful, loving, and hospitable seemed to be the theme of our Ireland trip and the thesis for our marriage. The hitchhikers were French ice-cream makers, and they did not murder us, a very favorable outcome, especially since they invited us to their creamery whenever we wanted to visit. While dropping them off, we couldn't get over just how perfect the day had been, especially that we had found the Brennan grave.

"Mom, mom—guess what! We found the Brennan grave!" I nearly screamed over Skype to my mom. "It took a while, but we prayed over it and thanked them for coming over to America!"

"Oh, Matt, that is so nice—I didn't know you were visiting County Kilkenny too?!"

Apparently, my Brennan ancestors were from the town of Clough in County Kilkenny, not Waterville in County Kerry. We had spent the day traipsing through two cemeteries seeking out the wrong family's name at churches and cemeteries that no relative of mine named Brennan had probably ever set foot upon.

"It was the Sheas who were from Waterville," said my mom.

"Huh," I remember thinking, and for a split second I thought maybe the day was a complete waste of time. But it's hard to think of any day as a waste when you're remembering and praying for a complete stranger. Prayers are never wasted, and the respect one pays for the dead never goes unnoticed, in my opinion. Perhaps there was even a humorous moment in heaven when the Waterville Brennans chuckled from above, sending pints of heavenly Guinness to the Kilkenny Brennans in gratitude for the misappropriated afternoon of remembrance and prayer by their Coke-drinking great-great-grandson and his patient and sweet wife.

While the family tree in my mind certainly needed fertilizer, the branches were strong and the roots felt firm.

23

No Sympathy for the Devil

On a beautiful mid-May Monday at Harvard University, researchers were working on mapping the brain to improve treatment for Alzheimer's. Professors were hoping to better the lives of learners in some of the most disadvantaged school districts across the country. Law students were providing pro bono services to entrepreneurial start-ups. A young woman from Latin America was talking about how she was going to run for office.

Sadly, none of this was front-page news. Instead, the media was talking about a small group of students, part of the Harvard Extension School Cultural Studies Club, who were planning to host a mockery of the Catholic Mass by putting on "black mass," which involves the desecration of a consecrated host. Reading the details of what happens at a so-called black mass bothered me in more ways than one.

As a Harvard grad and employee, and as a Catholic, I was reluctant to react in public. I felt torn in deciding how to act and what to say. There have always been issues I've had with Mother Church and issues I've had with Mother Harvard. Organizations led by people are inherently flawed, and as a member of both communities, it is not likely that I would ever be perfectly happy with all of their decisions. In general, I support the core tenets of both the Church and Harvard, but this black mass put me in a special position as someone associated both publicly and privately with the Church and the university.

Friends and colleagues asked me how I felt about this, and for a while, I really didn't know how to articulate my feelings. On the one hand, I am a firm believer in freedom of expression, freedom of worship, and freedom of speech. But in the case of the black mass, I struggled to understand how a mockery of something sacred to others could be an authentic expression of belief. In situations like this, I have often been drawn to the Serenity Prayer: "God grant me the serenity to accept the things I cannot change, the courage to change the things I can, and the wisdom to know the difference."

For me, the rub was in knowing what I *could* change.

Could I change this black mass from happening? What could I say or do that hadn't already been voiced? Would I just be joining the chorus of angry "Dear President Faust" letters, or would mine be the one that made a difference? Were my outrage and frustration exactly what the hosting organization wanted?

Countless Serenity Prayers led me to a mantra that would be part of how I would address the situation: *I am going to love the hell out of those I dislike.* I would love all those people who were desecrating Jesus and promoting religious intolerance, and I would not feel hatred toward the Satanic Temple planning to perform the ritual, the Cultural Studies Club that was hosting the event, or anyone at Harvard for letting this happen. Jesus might say, "Father forgive them, for they know not what they do." I would like for him to add, "Father, help me to love those that are hard to love." I discovered that this act of loving those we might want to hate is where the courage component of the Serenity Prayer comes in. The triumph of love, in communion with other followers of Christ, is the greatest weapon against evil.

In fact, I wasn't the only one who felt this way. Catholics, Christians, and allies—religious and atheist—from across the Harvard campus and beyond had planned a vigil and prayer service to occur simultaneously with the black mass. Harvard would be alive with prayer and joy and love, with religion in the air and the presence of godliness and goodness ubiquitous, regardless of what else would happen.

This vigil was something I needed to participate in and witness. I checked the website of St. Paul's Church to find that there would be a Eucharistic procession happening from the Massachusetts Institute of Technology campus to the Harvard campus, ending in a prayer service at St. Paul's, Harvard's main Catholic hub in the community. Most Eucharistic processions I had been part of up to that point were ceremonial and tied to a festival, and therefore very much pro forma, "we do this every year at this time" sorts of events. This one was quite the opposite—it was a very public march through the streets, and participants would bear witness to what they believed in. It would also serve as a peaceful, loving response to the black mass that was supposed to happen on campus that night. I scoured the Internet for information about the procession and made a few phone calls, but I could not determine exactly the route it would take.

So, I rode my bike to Harvard Square, locked it up, tied my shoes, and decided to look for the Eucharist as I walked around the main thoroughfares from Harvard to MIT. My goal was to meet the procession halfway and join the group on the way back to St. Paul's.

I had lived in Cambridge for many years at that point and knew the best routes from one spot to the next. Checking my iPhone and Twitter feed for both updates and shortcuts, though, I was having the hardest time meeting up with the procession. I saw news vans zoom past me and photographers walking around too. I saw people stationed on the side of the street with vigil candles and religious iconography, and I passed women praying and singing in Spanish, Vietnamese, and Haitian Creole. It was clear I was on the perceived parade route, but no parade was in sight.

I kept walking and walking and walking, yearning to be part of the procession. It was getting close to the point at which the vigil was supposed to start, which generated fears in me that, somehow, the procession had taken some strange route to St. Paul's and I had missed it and was missing the vigil too.

I gave a few more streets a quick glance, then decided to jog back the way I had come, hoping to end up at the church on time. Sure enough, as I pulled up on foot, so did Harvard's president Drew Faust, who was heading into the church in support of this unified Christian voice. Still confused as to how I had missed the procession, I grabbed an aisle seat in the last row and decided to wait. The church was already packed, and a steady stream of new faces entered from all the doors like Grand Central Terminal at rush hour. As friends and colleagues streamed in and sat beside me, I was overcome with a sense of the collective strengthening of the spiritual soul of the Harvard community. Harvard often gets a bad rap for being a godless place, and yes, hosting black masses in the name of free speech on campus doesn't help that reputation, but the vigil at St. Paul's represented the perfect counterpoint to any assertion that God is dead in liberal cities or colleges across the Northeast. We were all there to support that which we held sacred in a peaceful and prayerful way.

Like many churchgoers before him, Jesus was fashionably late that night . . . When the procession did arrive, there was a sense of awe like I had never experienced: the incense crept into the vestibule, and the quiet whispers reverberating through the church came to an abrupt halt—like when a conductor picks up his baton before a symphony. Everyone in attendance, in that giant church packed to the brim, was not angry or mad but strengthened by one another's presence and by the arrival of Jesus.

"Thank you all for coming tonight. I would like to share news that the 'black mass' that had been scheduled for tonight on the Harvard campus was canceled," one of the priests announced.

It turns out the club had tried to move the event off campus but could not find a place to host the black mass. There are mixed reports about whether a few members of the New York–based Satanic Temple actually held the black mass, possibly in a local bar although an employee of the bar mentioned he didn't see any rituals being performed, just Temple members drinking at the bar.

The prayer service was a powerful testament to a peaceful and loving response to hate. Yet amid all the excitement of that night, I couldn't help but chuckle over how it began, not being able to find Jesus on familiar roads and routes in a city I knew so well. It seemed an appropriate metaphor for my previous year, with spiritual meandering, glancing around, seeking council in the route, and eventually returning on a journey that I thought I knew. In this era of Google Maps and Twitter, the Bible and the Beatitudes, we do not always know the way, and we must keep faith in the journey. Besides, we can trust that Jesus will always come home.

24

Semiretirement

Some refer to it as Catholic Disneyland—the Shangri-La of all the most novel, noteworthy, and kitschy Catholic commodities across the country. For vendors, speakers, authors, and educators, it is the Olympics, Super Bowl, and Vatican Easter Vigil all tied into one special week. It is also *the* place to be for a guaranteed spotting of Fr. Jim Martin, SJ. It is held in Anaheim, California, at the convention center next to Disneyland, and its logistics and coordination require two full-time, year-round staff members and hundreds of volunteers. To those who attend, it is sacred, and to those of us who have only heard of it, it's the stuff of legends. To me, the Los Angeles Religious Education Congress is the ultimate speaking venue.

"Do you miss doing talks?" Nell asked as we were chatting over dinner one night.

I had greatly scaled back my time as a speaker, conference presenter, and TV writer in the year following my surgery and broken foot. I had stepped away from the grind of producing three-minute *A Word with Weber* videos for the CatholicTV network, which I had produced weekly for the previous three years. I was only occasionally accepting speaking offers, and I did my best to take it easy, in hopes of minimizing stressful scenarios that might induce future ulcers and stomach problems. I considered myself semiretired at the ripe age of thirty, pleased with the success of my stint as a Catholic media personality and contented with working full-time as director of digital communications strategy at the Harvard Graduate School of Education, and learning how people not on book tours fill their weekends. Nell and I took sailing lessons on the Charles River, I started cooking with heirloom tomatoes we had grown ourselves, and I was even beginning to dive into the surprisingly interesting art of birding. After a long day, I would take our kayak out on the Mystic River and creep up on the most beautiful blue herons I had ever seen. Their grace and the majesty of their flight was the antithesis of how I danced at our wedding.

I was happy and at peace, but I still had that itch—that itch that can only be scratched when you know you are doing something for a reason greater than yourself.

"I do miss speaking to groups about my faith, but I don't want to kill myself again," I said.

"Then get back on the horse and share your story. You're good at it and you love it. And if you die, I'll kill you," my wife quipped.

A slight nudge was all I needed to get my butt in gear. But this time, I didn't really know what to say any more. It had been close to two years since my last book came out, and I felt as if I had shared that message enough times already. I was ready to find something new to talk about.

"Whatever you write your next book about, make sure it's something you really want to talk about for the next year. Something you care deeply about, something you want to explore and understand better," said a friend of mine in the publishing industry.

Perhaps it was the quiet afternoons on a kayak looking at the plumes of swans, herons, geese, and all the other majestic birds on the river, but I really didn't have much to say at that time. At my peak, I was producing the video essays for CatholicTV every Monday, writing a weekly op-ed for Busted Halo, giving talks across the country on the weekends, and occasionally appearing on the radio before 7 a.m. on the weekdays. My brain had been in a constant state of creativity, and I was conditioned to connect my daily living with broader messages, messages I would then bring to the media I was producing. What worried me when I thought about going back on the road was that I was afraid it might bring me dangerously close to the stressful lifestyle I had so recently lived.

And then, to quote Michael Corleone, "right when I thought I was out, they pulled me back in":

Dear Matt:

I hope that you are doing well and enjoying the first week of summer. Your name was recommended to us as a possible presenter for our annual event known as the Religious Education Congress, taking place the weekend of March 13–15, 2015. We are interested in having you as a presenter, but before a formal letter of invitation can be sent, we must complete a process on our end . . .

Blessings . . .
Jan C. Pedroza
Archdiocese of Los Angeles

I had been asked to speak at the 2015 Religious Education Congress in Anaheim, and somehow, through some stroke of good luck, they accepted me. To a kid who went to Catholic schools his whole life, had an aunt who was a nun, had multiple priests at every birthday party, and was an eight-year veteran of altar serving, getting the nod to be a speaker at the Religious Education Congress was like getting to ring the bells, carry the cross, *and* light the paschal candle at the Easter Vigil. It was heaven on earth! I immediately accepted and was asked what my topic would be. I left my title and description purposely vague so I could figure out exactly what it was I would say:

Renewing Young Adult Catholic Imagination

Reflecting on twenty consecutive years of Catholic schooling, Harvard humorist Matt Weber shares his story of overcoming the myriad challenges that come with being a twentysomething Catholic in an increasingly secular world. Both inspiring and entertaining, Weber brings energy and joy to the new evangelization with his public witness as the "Andy Rooney of CatholicTV." This unique approach of connecting young Catholics to a renewed faith perspective prompted CBS News to call Weber "the voice of a new generation of Catholics."

The description included a bit of my usual go-to, not-so-humble-but-hopefully-true facts about myself, sprinkled with a heavy dose of generic marketing language, but I had purposely left things ambiguous so I could allow myself time to decide what it was exactly that I wanted to share. And so, like an old, out-of-shape Rocky Balboa in great need of training, stair running, and spiritual meat pounding, I began to prepare for the big show. What I would say, though, I really hadn't a clue . . .

25

Wisdom

When sitting down in a shower, you have to make sure the water is extra hot. The pseudo-science behind it is simple: water comes out hot and immediately cools off when hitting the air. The longer it is in the air, the cooler it gets. When standing, the water typically hits your body immediately upon leaving the spout, providing that refreshing burst of warmth that one becomes accustomed to when showering. When *sitting* in a shower, however, the water leaving the faucet must travel an additional three to four feet until it comes into contact with your head, and since the air has naturally cooled the previously hot water, it leaves those who choose to sit with a less enjoyable, warm shower feeling.

These are some of the thoughts I have in the shower. These and many others since I find some of my best thinking occurs while I'm relaxing in the shower. For me, this is a time with no agenda, a safe place, and one of extreme privacy and comfort.

"You OK, Matt?" my wife yelled from the other room. I knew I was spending too much time in my "office" when my wife began to check on me and the water got cold, having depleted the fairly generous reserves in our hot-water heater.

What *did* I care about? What did I want to talk about? What seemed meaningful to me? What message could I send that might help people? I looked around at our little bathroom: fresh paint on the walls, some fancy scented candles Nell had bought, some cracking caulk, a few split tiles, and a brownish grime that reminded me I needed to scrub the tub. I saw all of this from my low vantage point. Behind me on the ledge were leftover bottles of Tums, Prilosec, and Pepto-Bismol, all of varying levels of fullness. A ratty terry-cloth inflatable bath "pillow" was strewn in the corner; it had once cradled my broken left foot that could not get wet. I looked down at the giant red line on my body that went from sternum to belly button, and that along with the suture holes, resembled a pinkish zipper tattoo.

"Matty?" called Nell, slightly louder this time, looking to make sure I hadn't turned into a raisin.

"Yes, sweetie! I'm fine." I was actually more than fine: it had dawned on me what I could and should talk about at the Religious Education Congress. All the signs were around me, on me, in me, and audible to me. That once-hot, then-cold shower of life was rebaptizing me as I lay naked, vulnerable, and open to the rawness of the emotions that had been stewing inside of me—the pain, the anger, the sadness, the perspective, the ups and downs, the love, the joy, the prayers, the healing, the regrets, and the biting hope I had yet to shake.

I firmly believe my physical, emotional, and spiritual mettle had yet to be truly tested until that troubled year. And the result of it all was a later-in-life introduction to grit and resilience through a crash course I never would have designed, or even imagined. I was by no means tough, but that year was my first experience with getting tough, with coming out on the other side rougher and with a few calluses on the soul. If a naive, wussy person like myself somehow ended up beaming from ear to ear while sitting in a cold shower, incredibly touched that his wife didn't want him to turn into a raisin, then perhaps some of what I had learned could help others. Maybe even in sharing some of those stories, both good and bad, the lessons and learnings from my last year could be of value for others in the form of publicly swapping scar stories—the best of times, the worst of times, in sickness and in health.

With that properly watered idea and a few subsequent brainstorms in my office, I was ready to head back to California for yet another redemptive comeback trip, but hopefully with different outcomes. My wife could not make it, but she made me make one promise: "No jumping off stages!"

I was the last speaker on the last day of the conference. My time slot was the eighth period, and from what I gathered, it was the spot where many of the newbies were placed. While this gave me time to prepare upon arrival, it also gave me extra time to get sick, get nervous, overprepare, and see how good so many of the other first- through seventh-perioders were. I found myself sampling the conference the first two days like the way my mother describes going to the 1967 World's Fair in New York. There we were celebrating a faith tradition more than two thousand years old, but it felt modern and fresh, and the energy and excitement in the convention center was palpable. I passed a vending machine fully stocked with votive candles. Every religious order seemed represented, and I was in awe of the variety of robes and habits worn by their members. At any given moment, I heard at least three different languages spoken, yet everyone shared the same nonverbal language of smiling.

I judged it to be a good, happy crowd, and that eased my nerves, at least a little. The day and hour finally came when it was time for me to head in to the ballroom. I had gotten there early to check on the microphone and to check in, but I was too afraid to sit there and nervously wait to see if anyone would come. After all, in the grand scope of all the speakers, I was the equivalent of St. Polycarp—a nice guy who no one knew anything about.

"Are you the speaker?" someone asked as I sat on what I hoped was an out-of-the-way chair outside the ballroom, trying to remain incognito until the last moment.

"Yes, I am."

"Well, I can't make it to your talk because there is a really good talk happening this period too down the hall."

Comforting. Not only was I unknown and random, but also I was competing with a "really good talk" too. Well, in two hours, it would be over, and I could slink back into retirement and back to the stimulating world of birding on the Mystic River.

"Well, wish me luck," I said to the nun sitting in the hall across from me, as I got up and dragged my feet into the ballroom.

"Luck! I won't wish you luck! I'll pray for you! You don't need luck when you have God," she quipped back, smiling. Her words were exactly the verbal and spiritual nourishment I needed.

"Even better. Thank you!" I responded.

As I walked into the ballroom I overheard some giggles from women in the area just inside the door. I'm sure they were wondering why I would ask a nun for luck, when nuns are usually willing and able to offer a prayer. I smiled as I walked into the room, took the stage, and looked out over what was the largest crowd I had ever spoken in front of.

At peace, prepared, and knowing I had just received a much-needed blessing from a professional blesser, I felt good—a less flabby Rocky Balboa with gloves tightened, shoes laced, and mouth guard in. And for the following fifty-nine minutes, I delivered a roller-coaster ride of my first year of marriage, also my favorite and least favorite year of my life. Like the previous talk in California, things were going well, and I was once again overflowing with hope and the Holy Spirit.

I recited:

> May the road rise up to meet you.
> May the wind be always at your back.
> May the sun shine warm upon your face; the rains fall soft
>   upon your fields and until we meet again, may
>   God hold you in the palm of his hand.

I was an O'Donnell now, so ending with an Irish blessing seemed natural. Then I continued:

"But speaking of being in the palm of one's hand: you know how they say when you fall off your horse (or a stage) it's good to get back on? Enough time has passed, and if you're feeling as much joy in your heart as I am today at this conference, let's see if God's music comes through us."

Reaching into the front pocket of my suit jacket, I pulled out a shiny harmonica. I did not take requests. I knew what I would play. Every ounce of my body, heart, and soul was oozing with joy, and an ode to that ecstasy needed to be played.

And so for the last minute of my talk, I played "Ode to Joy" from the stage of a ballroom at the Anaheim Convention Center. Stepping down the stairs while still playing, I jigged, kicked, and danced to my own music. I was almost outside myself as I made it halfway down the aisle, still playing, only just then noticing a sudden influx of iPhones and other devices pointed right at me.

It was a freeing moment as the music, the Spirit, and the energy of the room overcame me. I danced back up the stairs to the front of the stage, with just a few notes to go before the song was over.

I'm going to jump, I thought to myself. *I can make it. The stage is a little higher, but it will be an epic way to close out the talk, finally sticking the landing at a Catholic conference in the state of California. I can do it. I'm going to do it.*

My toes were literally hanging off the stage. I looked up at the crowd, bent my knees, and gave every indication I was about to stage dive yet again, with my trusty harmonica along for the ride.

There are few moments in life when we can actually pinpoint a definitive gaining of wisdom. In this case, it was in front of hundreds of people, on the edge of a stage, as they saw a gangly, six-foot-three harmonica player take a step back, finish the last note, and then thank them all for coming. I'm sure if I had jumped, I would not have broken my foot again. In fact, I was quite certain I could've landed safely. But I feel a certain grace in knowing that I kept a promise: to my wife, but also to myself: to learn from the past, take risks when necessary, and know not to confuse adrenaline with the Holy Spirit.

The next afternoon, while sitting poolside and picking at fancy hotel French fries, Tom McGrath, a dear friend of mine from Loyola Press, and I looked at notes from my talk and began to sketch out this very book.

26

The Beautiful, Basic, and Boring

Perhaps in the same manner of reading books, writing books is often done in one's underwear. With a less frenetic, eternally faithful pooch nestled next to me, and my stalwart wife bookending me on the couch, most summer evenings have been fat and quiet with writing as the featured billing.

"If you write one thousand words tonight, I'll run out and get you a pizza from Figs," said Nell in her best sales-pitchy voice.

Figs is my favorite pizza place. It does not deliver, and it's a bit of a drive, but how blessed was I that my wife knew exactly what it takes to motivate me, feed me, and nourish my soul?

When I finish writing for the night, our favorite place to be on a Friday is sitting on our couch and watching something funny—lately it's been a good Steve Martin film. Weekend plans usually involve a few errands here and there, and visits with friends we don't see during the week, but our weekends are purposely unstructured, with little that we *need* to do aside from going to Mass. We sit quietly, happily at home, and many a blissful evening feels like a peaceful two-person retreat. We make soup. We heat up a few homemade crepes, alternating between brown sugar with butter and Nutella. I walk the dog and usually call my parents to check in on them and hear about their day. The walk and talk ends, and Nell and I slowly doze off, depending on how familiar we are with Steve Martin's antics; in many ways, we are doing everything we want by doing nothing, and we couldn't be happier.

In the mornings, I paint. She works on the garden. We hold hands on the walk to church. I pick out the ripe avocados at the supermarket. She recycles the junk mail. She fixes the broken ice machine in our fridge. I bring leftover cookies to the neighbor boys across the street.

The basic and the ordinary, the non-bookworthy minutiae of a typical day is now the extraordinary that I seek in life. It is what I hold sacred and dear, and it flows in the marrow of my bones. It is not sexy or spectacular, but deserves some love just for its simplicity and peace. I am still totally head over heels for my wife, and revel in the fact that I wake up next to my best friend every morning. She is my Bible verse, my daily Scripture, and my walking reminder to be good and do good. Through her witness and everyday example, Nell allows me to experience God's goodness and graces in new ways, and strengthens my transformed relationship with God in a deeply intimate and personal way. The God and girl I knew at my twenty-ninth birthday party are not the God and girl I knew at my thirtieth or thirty-first. A sacrament, a surgery, a shower, and a C harmonica were all part of the journey into my third decade of living. As T. S. Eliot famously said: "We had the experience but missed the meaning. And approach to the meaning restores the experience in a different form."

If you take away just one thing from this book, I hope it is this: *find the meaning.* It may not be present in the moment or immediately along the route you choose to explore or experience. It often needs time to marinate and percolate. It may be hidden in dead birds, mistaken identities in Irish cemeteries, or in fart clouds confined under hospital blankets. For me, the blur and busyness and pain and self-pity were initially all I could see. Once out of the haze, though, far enough removed from the experience, clarity and light have become more visible. While still fragmented, harnessing that light and shining it upon my past and present allowed me to better navigate the future—and if you take the time to pause and look, it can do that for you too.

And so, in my underwear, I write the last words of this book, which was formerly a conference presentation and a muddled series of telling fortunate and unfortunate life events. Having stewed on it all for many, many months has allowed me to truly relive the experience, sometimes painful and sometimes joyous. But seeing my life in a different form, now on the page, has helped me make some sense of it all so that I may grow in wisdom, and I hope this helps you connect to some episode, experience, or moment of your own. Wisdom seeking is a team sport, and I highly recommend finding a companion—a road-trip buddy or two—for the journey. Whether they are sleeping or navigating, such communion is vital for the trip, since love will fuel any journey wherever it needs to go.

Precisely 1,107 days after looking up at those hazy Houston stars and quietly whispering to God my hopes for an exciting year, I find that same brightness and guiding light in the glimmer of my wife's eyes. How blessed am I to have met her and been reintroduced to God through her, in a year of profound transformation and learning to not always jump for joy.

Epilogue

by Nell Weber

When I look back on that year—our first year of marriage—*of course* I remember Matt being sick. I remember where the nurses kept the heated blankets in case he got cold. I remember coming home alone after the nighttime staff kicked me out. I remember making him milkshakes every night so he could begin to gain back the weight he had lost. I remember cheering when he had a successful visit to the bathroom. But mostly, I remember that year as the first, early days of a big new phase in my life—one in which I was no longer primarily someone's child, or a (sometimes selfish, I'll admit) independent single woman—but a phase in which I was a partner, a spouse, a wife.

As I write this, we're still newlyweds—at least by my definition! We've been married only two and a half years, and I can't say that the wonder and joy at getting to spend each day with your dearest friend, your biggest supporter, and your most adventuresome challenger has worn off. It's still the best! And I hope it will be always. That year for us *was* an adventure, full of many, many fun memories and also some experiences that tested our mettle. However, through it we were able to see parts of ourselves and parts of each other that usually take decades of knowing someone to uncover. I feel sad that Matt had to suffer so much, but I feel grateful to know that we are fully capable of weathering storms together.

Matt loves Bob Dylan, and one of his favorite songs is "Shelter from the Storm." In the song, a nameless "she" provides shelter to the narrator, who has been wandering in the storm-filled wilderness. If you ask Matt, maybe that's what he would say I was doing. But the hardest thing for me as I read a draft of this book was reading how he wrote about my role in taking care of him that year.

Matt seems to think that I did something noble or sacrificial by caring for him when he needed me. I want to tell him, "But you just don't understand!" Honestly, and I promise with no false modesty, I need to tell you that I mostly just watched and loved as my darling husband was hurt and then healed himself, and throughout he continued to be the charming, cheerful, optimistic man that he is.

I did just what someone does—and should do—for their loved ones; it's just that most couples don't experience such serious health problems so early in their time together and at such a young age.

So, as much as I love Bob Dylan, the way I see it, Ray LaMontagne's got it right. In his song with the same theme, "Shelter," the narrator and his love promise to shelter *one another*.

Our first year of marriage wasn't about Matt's illness, but learning how to look after each other during some of life's storms—the physical ones, the spiritual ones, and even those hyperlocal, foul-smelling "storms" that emanate from your husband's backside.

Together they had overcome the daily incomprehension, the instantaneous hatred, the reciprocal nastiness, and fabulous flashes of glory in the conjugal conspiracy. It was time when they both loved each other best, without hurry or excess, when both were most conscious of and grateful for their incredible victories over adversity. Life would still present them with other moral trials, of course, but that no longer mattered: they were on the other shore.
      —Gabriel García Márquez, *Love in the Time of Cholera*

Acknowledgments

I am deeply grateful for all the love and support in both surviving a difficult year and managing to write something about it. Special thanks to my touchstone, tireless parents, John and Peggy Weber, who are my total heroes; my pesky, loyal, and supportive sisters, Kerry Weber-Lynch and Liz Begley, who always make sure I get extra pickles at Friendly's; my mother-in-law Mrs. James O'Donnell, whose generosity and love are commensurate with the Southern state in which she resides; my wonderful brothers-in-law, Jeremiah, Colm, Hall, and John; and my goddaughter Cordelia, whose smile could bring world peace.

At Loyola Press, I must first thank Tom McGrath and Joe Durepos. Tom, for birthing this idea and nurturing it in its adolescence, and Joe for raising it, forming it, and teaching it to find love. These two men are the reason this book is in print today, and I am eternally grateful to them for not just their professional help but also their valued friendship over the years. At Loyola Press, I must also thank my terrifically percipient editor, Rosemary Lane, meticulous copy editor Katherine Faydash, and a fantastic staff of mission-driven employees: Becca Russo, Andrew Yankech, Ray Ives, Carol Dreps, and Vinita Wright. To the publisher, Fr. Paul Campbell, SJ, too, I thank you all.

At Harvard, I wish to thank the entire community that supported me, loved me, and welcomed me back with open arms time and time again: Mike Rodman, Fernando Reimers and Eleonora

Villegas-Reimers, Lory Hough, Iman Rastegari, Meredith Lamont, Nate Hinchey, Mark Robertson, Patricia Brown, JoAnn Sorabella, Mohan Boodram, Rilda Kissel, Matt Tallon, C. Chung, and James Ryan.

At CatholicTV, I am always indebted and grateful for the continued generosity and inspiration from Fr. Robert Reed, Jay Fadden, Helen Lee, Charles Green, Kevin Nelson, Adam Stone, Peter Kaminski, Bonnie Rodgers, Richard Brown, and the whole team.

Also I must thank all of the nurses, surgeons, and doctors who helped me heal during this trying year.

Finally, to the countless people who prayed for me or supported me during this process, including James Martin, SJ, Fr. Brian Shanley, O.P., Fr. Jeffrey Ballou, Lisa Hendey, David Chen, Christian "Octo" Mantoni, Douglas Jebb (DJfCT), Ken Mirvis, my Wisconsin relatives, Neil O'Donnell, Chris Motley, and my recently deceased family members, Marian Begley and Sr. Marie Martin, I thank you.

Am I forgetting anyone? Oh right, I suppose I should thank Nell. May her name bookend this book, in the same way she bookends my days.

About the Author

Matt Weber is a Harvard-educated humorist, called "the voice of a new generation of Catholics" by CBS News. He is the author of the acclaimed Loyola Press book *Fearing the Stigmata* (2012) and a national speaker, producer, and writer. In early 2015, Weber launched his own 30-minute show on CatholicTV called "The Lens"—a weekly, humorous recap of digital trends, culture, and newsworthy events in the faith community. Weber's day job is director of digital communications strategy at the Harvard Graduate School of Education. Prior to arriving at Harvard, Weber received an M.A. in Higher Education Administration from Boston College and a B.A. in American Studies and Film from Providence College. Weber is an International Radio and Television Society fellow, triathlete, and avid harmonica player. He lives in West Medford, Massachusetts, with his beloved wife.

Also by Matt Weber

Fearing the Stigmata
Humorously Holy Stories of a Young Catholic's Search for a Culturally Relevant Faith

In *Fearing the Stigmata*, twenty-something Matt Weber—a Harvard graduate, television producer, and certified rosary-bead carrier—employs his sharp wit, earnest candor, and gift for great storytelling to illustrate for young adult Catholics both the real challenges and the immense joys of publicly living out the Catholic faith.

The fact that Weber has discovered a way to have a deep, ever-growing faith life that also manages to be culturally relevant will offer hope to many currently disengaged Catholics in the 18-to-35 age range.

Paperback | 3736-2 | $13.95

Available from Kerry Weber

Mercy in the City
How to Feed the Hungry, Give Drink to the Thirsty, Visit the Imprisoned, and Keep Your Day Job

When Jesus asked us to feed the hungry, give drink to the thirsty, and visit the imprisoned, he didn't mean it literally, right? Kerry Weber, a modern, young, single woman in New York City sets out to see if she can practice the Corporal Works of Mercy in an authentic, personal, meaningful manner while maintaining a full, robust, regular life.

Weber, a lay Catholic, explores the Works of Mercy in the real world, with a gut-level honesty and transparency that people of urban, country, and suburban locales alike can relate to. *Mercy in the City* is for anyone who is struggling to live in a meaningful, merciful way amid the pressures of "real life."

Paperback | 3892-5 | $13.95

Other Available Titles

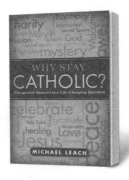

Why Stay Catholic?
Unexpected Answers to a
Life-Changing Question
MICHAEL LEACH
Paperback | 3537-5 | $14.95

What's So Funny About Faith?
A Memoir from the Intersection
of Hilarious and Holy
JAKE MARTIN, SJ
Paperback | 3739-3 | $13.95

The Thorny Grace of It
And Other Essays for
Imperfect Catholics
BRIAN DOYLE
Paperback | 3906-9 | $14.95

Continue the Conversation
www.LoyolaPress.com

If you enjoyed this book, then connect with Loyola Press to continue the conversation, engage with other readers, and find out about new and upcoming books from your favorite spiritual writers.

Visit us at **www.LoyolaPress.com** to create an account and register for our newsletters. Or scan the code below with your smartphone.

Connect with us through:

Facebook
facebook.com
/loyolapress

Twitter
twitter.com
/loyolapress

YouTube
youtube.com
/loyolapress